STARTING YOUR SMALL

GRAPHIC

DESIGN

STUDIO

Michael Fleishman

NORTH LIGHT BOOKS

Cincinnati, Ohio

Michael Fleishman is a freelance writer and illustrator whose stuff appears all over the place, for lotsa folks. The author of Getting Started as a Freelance Illustrator or Designer *and a contributing editor at* The Artist's Magazine, *he lives and works in Yellow Springs, Ohio. When he is not writing, painting or drawing, he tries to keep up with sons Max (age two) and Cooper (age four) and ahead of his wife, Joanne Caputo. He doesn't always.*

97 96 95 94 93   5 4 3 2 1

Library of Congress Cataloging in Publication Data

Fleishman, Michael.
    Starting your small graphic design studio / by Michael Fleishman. — 1st ed.
        p.   cm.
    Includes index.
    ISBN 0-89134-466-7
    1. Graphic arts — United States — Marketing. 2. Commercial art — United States — Marketing.
    3. Small business — United States — Management. I. Title.
NC1001.6.F64   1992
741.6'068 — dc20   92-26775
                                                          CIP

Edited by Mary Cropper
Designed by Carol Buchanan

The permissions on page 119 constitute an extension of this copyright page.

Acknowledgments

Where would I be without my family: Joanne, Cooper and Max — I love you.

Next, my gratitude goes out to Poppy Evans. Poppy, I was lucky to work with you!

My hat's off to one and all for your generous help, wealth of information, vast experience, expert advice and words of wisdom. You saw me through the slightly extended trek that led to the book the reader is holding now. Anyone somehow not mentioned in the text, you know who you are.

Thanks, Mary Cropper. Thank you, Lynn Haller! But of course, I need to acknowledge the hard work of all those good folks at North Light who nurtured, baby-sat and/or cattle-prodded this little opus into the real world.

It's all downhill from here, so finally, the author wishes to thank Susan Conner, who started it rolling.

Dedication

O.K. I want you to like my love and thank you for letting me love you. Yes, thank you for letting me love you.

— Written by Cooper Caputo Fleishman (age four)

Table of Contents

Chapter Five:
Pricing Your Work and Getting Paid

You have to make money to keep your studio running. Therefore, learning to price your work, propose a project to a client, get a good written agreement for the work, and then collect your money when you're done is vital to your success.

Chapter Six:
Managing Your New Studio

Getting off to the right start with a plan for tracking work on projects and for minding the store can prevent many sleepless nights later.

Chapter Seven:
Bringing in Clients

Feel good about selling creative solutions: find the clients you can help and show them what you can do, then keep them coming back for more.

Introduction

Starting a design studio can be a great adventure — or your worst nightmare. Your chances of success are better if you understand the problems you'll meet and work them out *before* you start. Many designers dive into a start-up on a wave of emotion. Some make it; some go under. Others flounder because they're intimidated by all the things they failed to consider before taking the plunge.

Perhaps you're a designer who's been on staff and is ready to go it alone. Maybe you're already a designer with your own office, but you began on the wrong foot and you would like to do it right the next time. Or you may be a designer just setting out, wanting to establish your own office immediately, but you're afraid you haven't got a clue how to go about it.

Starting Your Small Graphic Design Studio takes you step by step through the start-up maze. It will help you set out on the right foot and stay on track once you've opened your door. You'll find plenty of practical and creative ideas for every aspect of owning your own studio.

Inside the pages of this book you will find:

- Self-tests to tell you if you're ready for your own studio;
- Worksheets for planning your business;
- Forms, self-promotion pieces and planning materials from actual designers;
- Twenty-one case histories from designers with nuts-and-bolts information on how they got started and how they keep their studios working;
- Sidebars focusing on a variety of specialized areas of interest — plus much, much more.

While certainly an exciting experience, your new enterprise should not be a perilous ride down dangerous waters. And it's true that without the right directions you could easily lose your way. *Starting Your Small Graphic Design Studio* is your traveler's guide; use it to make the most out of this wonderful and thrilling journey. Let's get going!

CHAPTER 1

OFF ON THE RIGHT FOOT

Tired of working for others? Want the freedom to make your own design statement and name your own business hours? No longer care to bother with dress codes and office politics? Want to watch your kids grow up while you work at home? You'd like to create your own personal work space, pick and choose your projects, challenge yourself with bigger and better assignments? Would you like to be the boss, or be your own boss?

For whatever reasons, you have the itch to go out on your own, but do you have what it takes to succeed in your own design studio? It's a good question, and one we will explore in depth in this chapter.

A design studio can take many shapes and forms. A studio can be as small as a freelancer peddling graphics-related services such as typographic design, technical illustration, or even stats shot in her basement. Or it can be a megamillion, multidisciplined firm creating practically every type of graphic design imaginable, from packaging to environmental graphics.

For clarity's sake (and for the purpose of this book), let's define the basic term *design studio*: A design studio is an entity with a definite name and identity (something as straightforward as "Sue Jones, Freelancer" would qualify, as would the more esoteric "Chicken Soup Graphics"). Services include

total design, or carrying projects from concept to completion, rather than only single aspects of production (e.g., just doing paste-up). This design studio is one owned and operated by a graphic designer who works primarily out of his or her own place of business (either at home or a studio), not in someone else's studio, agency or graphic design department.

Regardless of whether you call yourself "Sue Jones, Freelancer" or "Chicken Soup Graphics," you are still going to be engaged in running a design studio. To make a go of it, you need to be a qualified professional and businessperson.

You may have purchased this book because you've been a practicing graphic designer for some

period of time and feel you have the know-how to tackle design projects on your own. Or you may be a student who doesn't want to work for someone else. Regardless of your place on the ladder, you know the basic steps involved in coming up with a design concept, presenting it to a client, and getting the job to printed completion. But one of the things you may not know is that the business of graphic design is one fraught with many complexities—all of which will be discussed and explained in this book.

Most designers reach a point where they begin to feel they could do it just as well as the guy they're working for. . . . There comes a time when maybe there's a disagreement in design philosophy or approach. And, as those differences become more and more uncomfortable, you decide it's not worth it—it's definitely time to either make a move or start your own business. We had already worked in all the best places in town, so moving to another studio wasn't an option. It was the appropriate time to go out and test the waters.

Don Sibley, Sibley/Peteet Design

Step 1: Do I Have What It Takes?

How do you *know* you've got what it takes to succeed on your own? The first step is to evaluate your design and business skills. The next is to evaluate the market for your services. The beginning of your entrepreneurial career—before you invest your time, energy and capital—is the best time to objectively assess your professional skills and personal qualities. I assure you, this is not as silly as it may sound at first reading. During a crisis, a bad year or crunch time, too many designers question their abilities (or worse yet, realize they don't quite have what it takes) and throw in the towel.

Evaluate Yourself and Your Experience

Be honest about who you are, what you can do and how well you do it. This won't necessarily prevent headaches, heartbreak or disasters, but it will give you a strong foundation to weather the storms that occur in the course of running your own studio. Answer this question by breaking it down into parts:

1. Since design is communication, are you an effective communicator?
2. Can you market your work and promote yourself, personally sell your vision to the client, and translate your client's needs into dynamic printed materials?
3. Someone goes to a specialist for something special—not pedestrian or cookie cutter graphics, but striking, thought-provoking, quality work. Are you a designer capable of leading the band rather than jumping on the bandwagon?
4. Do you understand (and not fear or loathe) the world of business and finance?
5. Experience makes a difference. Do you have enough? There is an advantage to starting with some experience instead of diving in right out of school. It is often easier to build business gradually as a moonlighter, while working full-time for someone else (some designers even get work from their employer's overload or turn-downs).
6. Are you going into business for the wrong reasons? You shouldn't be going into business for yourself if you are motivated entirely by ego. Don't do it if you're after fame, fortune or respect. And, last but not least, don't do it out of anger.

Evaluate Your Design and Production Skills

Knowing that you have the chops to do a job (and do it well) should be a given. To offer complete design services, you should be able to take a project through all phases of production (from conceptualization to completion), bring in and supervise support personnel and services if you need help, and make sure that all aspects of a project are done right. Your portfolio should reflect this by showing a variety of printed samples.

If you have worked for two or more years in a graphic design studio, advertising agency or even a

Yes No

Yes	No	
☐	☐	**1.** I can execute a flawless mechanical. I know how to efficiently prepare it and mark it up for a printer, color house or service bureau.
☐	☐	**2.** I can render a concept and present it to a client through thumbnails, roughs and comps.
☐	☐	**3.** I can come up with dynamite visual concepts on my own.
☐	☐	**4.** I can design just as well as or better than my competition.
☐	☐	**5.** I am quick and efficient in executing most design and production-related tasks.

publishing house, chances are that you've had some experience managing projects through all phases of production. You've probably had experience dealing with vendors, suppliers and freelancers, and have acquired a lot of the know-how necessary to run your own studio. Chances are, especially if this was a small studio, you've been aware of, if not directly involved in, the firm's day-to-day operations.

To determine if you have the design and production skills necessary for going into business on your own, see if the statements in the checklist on page 3 reflect your skills. Be honest—if you're lacking in any area, you can always work to develop additional skills or bring on a partner to supplement your abilities. Check *yes* only if the statement really does describe you.

If you're lacking in any of the areas, brush up on some of these skills by seeking the help of another designer, either for advice or hands-on assistance.

Evaluate Your Business Skills

The preceding questions are basic to the tasks involved in completing design projects. However, the questions you will be asking yourself next are crucial to running a successful business. You will need to practice salesmanship and learn basic accounting and business procedures—the kinds of things many college graduates know, but designers are least prepared for.

Yes No

1. I have good business communication skills. I am familiar with business etiquette and procedures when making written and verbal contact.

2. I can set reasonable goals and follow through on them.

3. I am able to get along with just about anybody and can motivate others to help me with what I am involved in.

4. I can sell an idea to a client.

5. I make decisions quickly and accurately.

6. I don't procrastinate. I work steadily instead of starting a project a few days before a deadline.

7. I can see and understand the whole picture. I don't concentrate on one thing while ignoring other aspects of a situation.

8. I have good organizational abilities. I can handle several projects at once and keep track of progress on each.

9. I can juggle the projects on hand while cultivating new business.

A lot of designers decide they want to go out on their own to have "freedom," to not have to answer to a superior, to pick and choose appealing design, and to design without much intervention. It rarely works out that way. There's always someone you seem to have to answer to. And it's usually a more immediate source than you're used to—the client who's paying the bill.

Don Sibley, Sibley/Peteet Design

In order to determine if you have the business and management aptitude necessary for going out on your own, see if you agree with the statements in the checklist on page 4. Again, if you're lacking in any area, you can always develop these skills — there are many courses and books on business management and marketing basics.

It really does take an amazing amount of discipline and drive to make it. If you don't have that, or if you're just accustomed to working for somebody else and you're a nine-to-five kind of person, the chances of really making it are pretty slim.

Rex Peteet, Sibley/Peteet Design

Evaluate Your Entrepreneurial Savvy

Juggling the financial end of your business along with design and production tasks is one thing, but subjectively appraising your individual strengths and weaknesses, and taking stock of your grit, determination and discipline are another.

In order to determine how you stack up, see if you agree with the statements in the checklist below (and be honest; you know yourself best).

What's Your Score?

Only you know the correct answers to the questions in our evaluation section. And as you'll need these abilities to make the business work, you didn't kid yourself, right?

Now it's time to tally the number of *yes*'s and *no*'s and see how they stack up against your potential for success. All the questions raise issues that are important to maintaining a business. If you answered *no* to only one item in each of the above three categories, chances are good that you can go it on your own without any help. But if you answered *no* to more than three questions or more than one in any single category, you may be taking on more than you can handle by yourself. Unless you feel you can cultivate these qualities on your own, consider finding a partner (or rep) to help in the weak areas.

Yes No

☐ ☐ **1.** I am confident about my design abilities. If my work is not appreciated, I can shrug it off and apply myself with confidence to other projects.

☐ ☐ **2.** I am a self-starter. Nobody has to tell me to get going.

☐ ☐ **3.** I am highly motivated. I can keep working on a project for as long as I need to complete it on time.

☐ ☐ **4.** I can concentrate on the task at hand. I'm not easily distracted from what needs to be done.

☐ ☐ **5.** I am persistent. Once I know what I want, or make up my mind to do something, almost nothing can stop me.

☐ ☐ **6.** I am in excellent health and have a lot of stamina and energy.

Step 2: Is the Opportunity to Succeed There?

You will need to evaluate your potential market. Is there a niche out there you think you can fill? While it's not best to have all your eggs in one basket, it's good to have at least one major client to rely on — do you already have this client lined up? Do you have some idea of the kind of work you will be doing and the compensation you can expect?

Determine Your Potential Market

What type of work do you think you will be doing, and who do you think will buy it? How many clients are out there? You need to get a realistic picture of what you do best and what you think you could be doing to get business.

To help guide you in this process, ask yourself the following questions:

1. What do you really like to do?
2. What kind of design makes you happy?
3. What's your idea of a dream job, and what would you do gratis (just to have that type of work or client)?
4. What's your design history? What were your biggest triumphs?
5. What were your most successful projects?
6. What were your near misses?
7. What were your biggest flops?
8. Who is your competition? Think about your peers and analyze their work.
9. How many other designers are out there doing the same thing you want to do for the same kind of clients? Realistically assess if you're able to provide better design or service than your competition. You don't want to spend valuable time where there's little chance of gaining any business. Be a tough (but objective) critic: Who blows you out of the water? Who is the cream of the crop? Be mindful of what the competition is doing and honestly evaluate yourself.
10. Are you in a position to fill a void that the competition is not filling?
11. What's your current reputation? What do clients and vendors believe you have going for you? On the street, what might people hear about you, think of you and your work; what work have they seen; where has your work been seen?

As nebulous as it all may be, determining where you stand may make the difference between getting a job offer or getting a "try again next time." You don't want to waste your time marketing stellar design capabilities to your local mechanic. However, if you have very little experience, you'll want to think twice about selling your services to the biggest corporations in town — you may not get beyond the receptionist. Until you've proven yourself, you're probably better off working as a freelancer with the design firms these companies are currently employing.

Love What You Do

Once you get an idea of how to make money, it's also important to be sure that this is the type of work you really want to do and will find fulfilling. Finding your niche involves finding something that you can do well and make a living at, too. To stick with it through both lean and green times means you must truly love your work.

If you're cranking out schlock for the bucks when what really turns you on is coming up with innovative ad concepts, you won't be happy for very long. You need to take care of your heart's desire as well as your livelihood if your business is going to thrive over the long haul. Look for the kind of clients who are willing to give you projects that will be personally fulfilling as well as the ones that provide easy cash.

> My direction . . . did not exactly track with the main thrust of the firm. . . . My vision, plus the challenge and future potential of interactive technologies didn't mesh with where the studio was going. . . . I had confidence that I could continue to define that vocabulary, possibly even ahead of the mainstream. I could establish a market by doing this kind of work well and having it work right.
>
> *Tom Nicholson, Tom Nicholson Associates, Inc.*

Where Are Your Potential Clients?

After you've taken stock of what you want to do and where you stand relative to others doing similar work, you'll have a better idea of where to direct your marketing efforts. But you also need to ask yourself some more specific questions about your design and production capabilities. What aspects of a job do you do best? Are innovative design concepts your forte, or is meeting impossible deadlines your strongest capability?

Likewise, if there's a particular area of design that you're strongest in, you need to think about what kind of clients are in greatest need of that skill. If you're good at logo and identity work, you're better off looking in the private sector—particularly new businesses. If you're best at print advertising, you're ob-

viously going to be knocking on the doors of all the local agencies.

Consider related areas to expand into, as well. If you're a great book jacket designer, expanding into book and brochure design may not make as much sense as considering poster design—essentially a blown-up version of what you're already doing. But if you've been doing brochures, annual reports and booklets, then magazine and book design would be a natural spin-off.

What's your design style? Is it flamboyant or is it better suited to an attorney's office? Is your work likely to look dated in a few years or does it have a traditional feel? Or do you have a diversified style—adapting the look of your work to suit the project at hand? The look of your work, and how well you can adapt it to the image a client wants to project, has a great deal to do

with where your work is best marketed. For example, your local fitness center isn't likely to be sold on portfolio samples with a decidedly sweet and feminine slant.

Research, Research and More Research

Study the creative directories and competition annuals and note the clients of those designers whose work you admire. Scan the Yellow Pages. Talk to your friends. Network with other designers. Window shop downtown. Really look at who is out there doing what jobs, and who is offering those plum assignments to whom. Where is design expertise needed; where is woefully inadequate design being done? Now evaluate—what clients and which assignments are in sync with your particular design vision?

After considerable thought, you should be able to come up with some answers that will give you an idea of how you compare with your competition, how others will perceive your work, and where to consider taking your portfolio. You might even get an idea of where your "market niche" is. You'll see how to find and cultivate this niche as you delve further into this book.

Your Current Clients

If you're currently employed but moonlighting freelance jobs, you have existing clients you can probably bank on, to some extent. Get a realistic picture of how much you can count on these clients in the future. Be frank—let them know you're considering going into business for yourself and want to know if they will continue to provide you with work.

Any client you have been working with under your current employer can be one of your clients, as long as you don't rob your employer of their existing business with this client. Can you perform a service for this client that your employer doesn't want to perform? Is this client looking to expand its business into an area in which your employer doesn't want to be involved? Let's say your employer specializes in designing annual reports and doesn't want to be bothered with the company newsletter a client is contemplating. There's no reason why you shouldn't have an opportunity to do this.

Ongoing projects like newsletters can be the mainstays for a new design studio. Check it out by gently probing for spin-offs from projects you are currently involved in. If you have a good relationship with a client who likes your work, go for it!

Making a Graceful Break With Your Current Employer

Many designers agree that the best way to start your own studio is by moonlighting while you're currently employed, and then making the break when you have enough freelance business to support yourself.

Among the designers to go this route is Lori Siebert of Cincinnati-based Siebert Design Associates. The editors of the magazine for which Siebert was art director encouraged her to freelance because they saw that the focus and energy she absorbed from her outside assignments showed up in improved design of their publication.

Siebert also benefitted from the additional exposure. "In order to get visibility, I did a lot of pro bono work for arts organizations," she explains, adding that these jobs were frequently high-exposure vehicles such as posters and concert programs.

Soon, Siebert built enough freelance business to start her own studio. She had also become the envy of many designers in the area who coveted her position at the magazine. When she left, the publisher had no problem replacing her with another talented newcomer.

New York City-based Tom Nicholson of Tom Nicholson Associates, Inc. also left his employer after expanding his skills to a level beyond the scope of the firm's primary business. He offers this advice on maintaining an appropriate perspective: "In principle, you're grateful for all your employer has done for you." Although he benefitted from the opportunity to grow while working for another, his employer retained all credit for any of his work done while on staff. "An employee's good work feeds the business and grants that designer the opportunity to do what he or she does best. You give your all, grow and learn, then you take that experience with you when you leave—it's an exchange."

Nicholson says that the best way to part company is by doing whatever is necessary to avoid disrupting your former employer's business. "It really comes down to business. Your employer doesn't take it personally that you chose to leave, and you shouldn't believe that 'he won't like me anymore.' But you should do your best to look out for your former employer's business needs and interests. If you, in good faith, are trying to do that, you will have a graceful parting."

Rick Tharp

Starting a Studio Right Out of School

Tharp Did It is the name of the four-person California design firm headed by Rick Tharp. And indeed, Tharp *did* do it—he graduated in 1974 from Miami University (in Oxford, Ohio), struck out on his own, and built a thriving design studio without any prior studio experience.

Tharp decided to set up shop in Los Gatos, California, a small town in the Santa Cruz Mountains about an hour's drive south of San Francisco. Prior to moving to Los Gatos, Tharp freelanced for a few short months in Atlanta. "I had my car, clothes, books and record collection stolen on the same day," Tharp remembers. "The only thing they didn't get was my portfolio. I took a vacation to California, saw Los Gatos and never left."

Recalling those early days of doing business, Tharp says that his existence was a meager one. "My only resources at this time were my homemade drawing board, a file cabinet, one Mickey Mouse telephone, $1,700 in personal savings, and excess fortitude," he says. "I had zero experience—I didn't

know what to charge or how to estimate my time in advance. I figured this out by asking colleagues and friends what they charged. Then I tried to set a fair price based on my experience and expertise within a limited range."

Tharp ended up with his own business largely by chance. "I didn't plan on being a freelancer for long—I thought I'd take a job or go into partnership with someone," he states. "But within a few months I had a portfolio of actual work. I knew I wanted to choose and control my own projects, so even though it was expensive, I established an office. My biggest expense was a stat camera," he says. "And I could have used more hours per day."

Despite the time crunch, Rick came through, and in those early days, Tharp did it by referrals and contacts. "I made connections through the Western Art Directors Club. I also sent promos to every ad agency and design studio in the area for freelance work, but found personal contacts to be more effective." Although he has developed a reputation for his award-winning

Tharp's promos may not appear to be keepers for him, but they are for his clients. He has seen the studio's promos decorating clients' offices many months and years after they were sent.

self-promotions, Tharp stresses the importance of personal contacts. "It has been very important to maintain a relationship with people who are successful and who we enjoy working with," he points out. "We have grown with most of our clients. Some have moved on to higher positions in other companies and we have moved up with them."

Although Tharp's earliest self-promotion pieces were aimed at getting new business from restaurants and retailers, he says that his current efforts focus on existing business contacts. "Now our promotional materials focus on retaining clients. Although most [of the materials] are of a humorous nature, they are all 'keepers,' and we have seen them in our clients' offices many months and years after sending them."

Tharp feels his start-up goals were very basic: "To do high-visibility work, and to do the best work I could—no matter what I was charging. Money wasn't a consideration. My services were based on hourly rates, but mainly on the value of the work to that particular client and application. These goals haven't changed much over the years."

Tharp has never worked for others (he says he still doesn't know what a paycheck looks like). "Until last year, I thought a three-figure income included the cents," he quips. But when this award-

winning (and decidedly self-made) designer is asked what words of wisdom he has for those going out on their own, he counsels: "Get a job in a small design firm to see, first hand, just how tough it is to run your own business."

Tharp Did It collaborated with a California winery to come up with this parody of the infringement of government regulations label design, Chateau LeWar'ning. The chateau logo, a bar code printed in gold ink, actually scans at supermarkets to reveal Tharp's phone number. The self-promotion, targeted specifically at wineries and breweries, was doubly successful for Tharp: Not only did it result in calls to review his studio's portfolio, it was further publicized in trade and consumer magazines.

Mike Salisbury

Putting Your Talents to the Best Use

"I was overqualified for a real job," Mike Salisbury says when asked why he wanted to go out on his own. "I went into business for myself for a variety of reasons — I was too fast and had too many skills to work at an agency and be adequately compensated or utilized."

Salisbury's multifaceted career began in 1962, when he was 20 and an art director for *Surfer Magazine*. "It was the first real job I had. The experience made me sort of a 'surf business-wiseman.' " Fired later that same year, he was soon hired at a retail advertising design agency. An award-winning illustration from Communication Arts in 1965 landed him an associate art director's position at *Playboy* magazine. This launched him on a series of short-term job assignments in a variety of positions, including art directing at United Artists Records, *Rolling Stone* and *West* magazines. He also had stints as a freelance designer and worked as a freelance photographer for *Esquire* and *Vogue*.

Salisbury confesses to a lot of hopping around in order to gain exposure: "I only took jobs as a way to advance my experience and portfolio. Money wasn't the issue; opportunity to learn and promote myself were my goals."

He was prompted to go out on

These mailers — which owe their continuity to their strong, simple design and the use of Salisbury's playful logo — keep Mike Salisbury Communications' clients posted on their agency's latest achievements.

his own in 1982, when he realized that his freelance work was bringing in more money than his paycheck as a creative director for a major advertising agency. "The first office of Mike Salisbury Communications, Inc., was my spare bedroom and one client (20th Century Fox). I then moved to a 500-square-foot office with an art student as my initial employee. At one time, I had up to 25 employees. My goal now is to cut back from 5,000 square feet to no more than 2,500. I currently have two employees and a bookkeeper. Everyone else comes in on a project-by-project basis. The computer and the recession have helped my decision to cut back on staff and office size."

As a result of spending 30 years working in the Los Angeles area, Salisbury was able to parlay his experience and many contacts (plus a whopping talent and grueling work ethic) into over a million dollars in billings his first year of business. His business continues to thrive today, but he qualifies his success with words of wisdom: "I think I have learned some valuable lessons . . . 1) Don't go into business without business; 2) You must promote if you want to eat; 3)Don't spend more than it takes to get the job done . . . ever; and 4) Don't do things you're not qualified to do (for me that's hand skills and bookkeeping skills)."

He pauses and adds this advice, "Work, study, learn and earn. And

don't burn any bridges — employers and employees can all turn out to be clients someday."

Thinking back to the start of Mike Salisbury Communications, Inc., Salisbury says, "I tried many times before making it — my goal for that first year was survival." With over a quarter of a century of great design behind him, he maintains that his goal for the next five years is still the same, "Survival . . . but with class."

This self-promotion piece suggests the range of Mike Salisbury's work — from his beginnings in magazine design to his television and movie work.

Tom Nicholson

Making the Break

It wasn't Tom Nicholson's intention to start his own design studio, Tom Nicholson Associates, Inc. Like most design school graduates, Nicholson immediately found a job after receiving his master's degree from Cranbrook Academy. As part of his position he got involved in exhibition design, which he describes as "a hybrid between graphic and industrial design. A graphic designer works in print and an industrial designer develops products for consumer use. Exhibition design combines aspects of each of these disciplines for communications in a public setting."

Nicholson soon found himself developing specialized skills and cultivating an expertise that was positioning him in an exclusive domain. "My direction didn't exactly track with the main thrust of the firm — or even the design world at large," he says. What made Nicholson's work different at that time (1982) was the relatively experimental work he was doing on the computer. "I design for the computer experience," he says. "You might know it as interactive video or multimedia. My vision for the potential of these interactive technologies didn't mesh with where the studio was going. If I wanted to continue to develop this infant discipline, I would have to do it as my own business elsewhere."

So in 1987, Nicholson made the break with his employer to go out on his own. "I set off cautiously," he explains. "But no matter how conservative you are, you are forced to completely sever all your support systems — you're giving it all up and starting over. For me, this was a huge leap of faith. There was no clear signal of a market to support this enterprise on its own.

"As an exhibition designer, I was working with clients who only knew that they had a communications goal and some money to put toward that goal. It was an 'artificial' market because it existed within the context of exhibition design — there was no interactive technology market by any means. We couldn't hang a shingle that said, 'We do interactive design.'

"I very consciously set certain business goals for myself," Nicholson says, "the first of which was simply to survive for one year and still be on my feet, independent and still serving clients. That's all that mattered — if I could do this, I had great confidence that I could grow the business from there.

"By the end of the year the basic life support systems were in place: an office, a small staff, an accountant, a legal advisor, paperclips — the simple necessities! But each of us had to wear more than just our design hats to keep this small office going. Our growth plan was based on the simple principle of sharing some of this load with each new hire as they arrived. In theory, this would allow us each more time to design." This process — six years later — has not stopped.

"I think I always knew," says Nicholson when asked how he determined he was ready for his own business. "It's something that people must look for inside themselves. I wanted to control my destiny. Coupled with that was the strong urge to rise or fall on my own merits. If I failed it would be because of me, not because of someone else. If I was successful, it would be because of my own efforts — I wanted to leverage my future opportunities."

Tom Nicholson's clean, classic letterhead design also works well for business forms such as this transmittal.

CHAPTER 2

CREATING A PLAN FOR YOUR BUSINESS

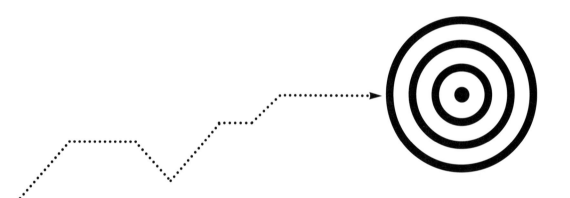

Now it's time to develop a plan detailing why you want to be in business, what you expect to achieve, and how you intend to make it all gel. We'll examine how you'll do what you do—whether it be working alone, forming a partnership or creating a corporation—and how to handle the sundry responsibilities involved (sales, client service, design time, production management).

We'll also discuss services you'll need to buy regularly (such as printing, photography, copywriting, stats, typesetting, etc.) and look at your present vendors, contacts to make, plus the cost of these services.

Step 1: Decide What You're Going to Do

This section, a combination wish list/mission statement, will help you evaluate your goals plus gauge your commitment, attitude and satisfaction from your chosen venture. Why do this little exercise? Your new business must be fueled by perception and passion as well as profits, otherwise it will certainly become a mere chore, or worse yet, a losing battle.

What Do You Really Want and Why?

Get in touch with yourself and your values. What's your perception of a successful business? Simply mak-

ing ends meet? Having the freedom to take time off and do your own thing as often as you wish? Or throwing yourself into a labor of love that will consume all of your time and energy?

Set goals that reflect your personal and professional values. In order to determine what you want and will be most comfortable with, ask yourself some questions. Write down your answers, and try to be as specific as possible in defining what you want. Don't edit yourself at first; just get your ideas down. Then review them for realism.

• **Why are you in this business and what are your personal aims?** Is it an extension of a hobby? Do you want more creative freedom and control over your design projects than you had under your employer? Do you want public or peer recognition for your work? Do you expect to make more money? Do you want financial security?

• **What are you putting into this enterprise—just your wallet, or your heart and soul?** Are you making a wholehearted commitment or just looking to get by?

• **What are your basic business objectives?** Do you want to break even after two years? Have 20 regular clients in three years? Increase billings 10 percent each year? Win at least five design awards per year? Make enough to pay bills and eat?

• **What do you want from your personal life?** Owning your own business is often a delicate balanc-

ing act. Your obligations to your family can have a profound bearing on the location of your business and on whether that business will serve a local or national clientele. A workaholic slaving away long hours at the studio (or a jet-setter with a hectic travel schedule) will surely miss out on the homefront.

It's important to be realistic about your personal expectations and abilities. If you're looking for security, starting a design business that is dependent on the talents of its owner is not the way to find it. Your business would immediately be in jeopardy if you became injured or ill and could not work.

A mission statement can play an important role in giving your studio direction. Bennett Peji's mission statement emphasizes his commitment to building long-term relationships with clients. "There is no more rewarding feeling in this business than seeing our clients' businesses grow with our help and have our business grow with them."

Set Goals

You've done some soul searching and you're in touch with your personal and professional aspirations. Now it's time to set goals that reflect those values.

• **Figure out what you need to earn.** You'll want to figure on making enough to meet your current salary level at some point in the near future. If you're the sole breadwinner in your household, this is especially important. Project yourself into the future and get an idea of what you want to be earning and when you need to attain this income level. If you've made a sizable investment in equipment and other start-up expenses, you'll also want to determine when the payback will be. In this chapter (and in chapter four) you'll find out how to draw up a financial plan to help you do this—but for now, get an approximate figure and date in mind.

• **Decide how much time to put into your business.** If you have

At the end of three years you must look at your business and ask, "Is there light at the end of the tunnel, or am I just fooling myself?" Then you must decide if it's worthwhile to continue.

Patrick Fiorentino, Pinkhaus

very few personal obligations, and are extremely ambitious, you may want to invest 50 to 60 hours a week. This would give you the opportunity to bill out a lot of your time, and still spend a large portion of it cultivating additional business. But if you have parenting obligations, you probably have some limitations imposed on your time already. Be realistic about how much time you can allot per week before you figure on where your business efforts are best spent.

• **Determine what your image will be.** Is it important to you to set a standard to which your peers will aspire? Do you want to do the

kind of cutting-edge design featured in the awards annuals? Or is your business a spin-off from a hobby—something with which to make some extra bucks?

If maintaining a high profile in the design community is very important to you, you'll want to set goals based on that aspiration. If you want to do trend setting work, you'll probably want the design freedom that comes with occasional pro bono work—paying clients frequently want what's safe and traditional, and they will pay only for getting the design they want, not the design you want. You'll have to determine what's most important. It's hard to do the kinds of design jobs that allow you to do the most expressive work (possibly pro bono) when you're trying to pay off the studio equipment you're currently financing. It's just as hard to make a sizable salary if you only have 30 hours per week to devote to your work.

Keep your overhead low. Keep everything really humble. . . . The worst thing you can do is go to the bank, borrow $100,000, print a letterhead, buy furniture, stamp machines, and commit to a big rent—then say, "OK, I'm ready for the work," and there's no work.

Tibor Kalman, M & Co.

Step 2: Decide How You'll Make It Work

Now you'll want to consider the basic configuration of the studio. Can you go it alone, should you take on a partner, or will you need to create a team? If you need people or services to supplement your design skills, how do you find them and where? You'll also be doing many tasks beyond design and production. There's a lot to do, somebody has to do it, and it must be done with organization.

Draft a Work Plan

One of the best ways to get a handle on how you're going to get started is to organize your time and prioritize the tasks that need to be done at the onset of your business. Divide the time that you spend into three basic areas:

1. Promotional: This category includes all activities you engage in while trying to obtain business. These activities include researching potential clients, time spent on self-promotional mailings, cold-calling, and designing your logo and business materials.

2. Billable: In this category is all time that can be billed to a client — every task and every aspect of completing a job that you know you will ultimately be paid for when a job is completed.

3. Administrative: Ongoing tasks including day-to-day, month-

Selecting a Lawyer

Don't wait for push to come to shove. Have your legal representative on call before you go into business. You'll also need this individual to draft papers of incorporation or partnership if you decide that you want to structure your business in one of these ways. Use the following guidelines when looking for a lawyer.

- Don't engage a "baby-sitter" to calm your jangled nerves. You need to hire a lawyer who knows his way around the courtroom. You want a lawyer who can draw up a bullet-proof agreement.
- Can we talk? Good communication skills are important. Your attorney should fully explain strategies and unfamiliar terminology and never sound patronizing.
- A referral makes for a nice lead, but not a blind decision. Shop around and interview three lawyers at least. Spend money on an initial consulta-

tion — it will be worth it in the long run.
- Avoid a lawyer who shuffles your case to a junior partner after your interview.
- If the lawyer is not upfront about his or her billing of services, don't hire him. When a case is closed or terminated, an honest lawyer will return unused portions of the retainer you pay at the start of the case.
- Don't hire a litigation-happy barrister. You don't need or want a Perry Mason "wannabe." If an attorney says he rarely settles out of court, he may prolong your case and drain your wallet.
- Study the lawyer's contract. Negotiate terms, if need be, and don't be in a hurry to sign.
- If he makes the point that he's "too busy," "swamped" or "overworked," forget the guy. Move on to your next interview.

to-month things like paying bills, invoicing clients and running errands are considered administrative tasks.

Now come up with a yearly plan. Analyze where your time is needed and for how long. You'll want to factor in more time for acquiring

business when you're just starting out — you won't be needing much time to complete projects if you don't have any clients, right? You'll also want to allow for more administrative time while you're setting up shop — for instance, looking for studio space, buying equipment

There's a feeling of isolation and loneliness — you have nobody to interface with or consult with. . . . There's also a tendency to become compulsive — to feel guilty about taking time off. One has less time for a social life.

Mary Nichols, Nichols Graphic Design

and setting up accounts.

Then break your yearly plan into twelve monthly plans that include a realistic projection of where your efforts will be best spent, and how much time you'll spend in each area. You may want to also take into account seasonal ebbs in the industry and vacation time. (Will August typically be a slow month and a good time to take a two-week hiatus?) The point is, organizing your priorities gives you a guide to where your time will be best spent, and allows you to project a goal for your gross income after a year of doing business.

To set up your monthly plan, start first with an idea of how you'll be spending your time on a weekly basis. For a start-up business, plan to spend 20 hours in promotion, 10 in administrative needs, and another 10 in billable hours within a 40-hour week. Multiply your weekly figure by four to get an idea of your monthly time allotment for each segment of your business. For example, out of 160 hours in a month, 80 would be spent in promotion, 40 in administration, and the remaining 40 in billable time. See the chart below for an example of a one-year projection.

A chart like this will also give you an idea of where you may need help. Let's say that after six months your promotional efforts are yielding more business than you ever dreamed possible. You feel that you're spending so much time cranking out work that you're robbed of the hours you need to keep track of billing and other administrative responsibilities. You'll know then that it's time to consider hiring someone part-time to help in production.

Charting time spent on billable hours will also give you an opportunity to set goals for your business income. If you spend 40 hours a month on your business at the onset, and you expect to charge an average of $50 per hour for your time, you can expect your income before expenses to be $2,000. Perhaps you've set a goal for an average of 100 billable hours per month. By the end of your one-year plan, at $50 per hour, you can look forward to hauling in $5,000 per month. Sound good? You bet!

Don't just work up these figures during your start-up period and then throw them in a drawer. Keep reviewing and refining them. If your plans aren't working, why? What do you need to do?

Drafting a Work Plan for Your Time			
	Promo	Billable	Administrative
Jan.	90	20	50 (setting up)
Feb.	80	50	30
Mar.	60	70	30
Apr.	60	70	30
May	60	70	30
June	60	70	30
July	50	80	30
Aug. (less 40 hrs.)	20	70	30
Sept.	40	90	30
Oct.	20	110	30
Nov.	20	110	30
Dec. (less 20 hrs.)	10	100	30

Here's an example of how a work plan for your time might look.

Choose a Business Structure

There are various legal and tax considerations involved in choosing a structure for your business. You may choose to establish a sole proprietorship, a partnership or a corporation.

If you're in business as a sole proprietor, the business is *you*. You personally garner all the profits and you personally are responsible for any losses, legal liabilities and business obligations. No formal papers need to be drawn up when you begin operation. You'll file a Schedule C: Profit or Loss from Business or Profession along with your 1040 come tax time. Your Social Security number acts as your business identification number.

In a partnership, profits, losses, legal liabilities and business obligations are shared. You'll want to draw up a partnership agreement and you'll need to obtain a federal ID number.

A corporation will safeguard you against personal liability. Legal action against Chicken Soup Graphics, Inc., is not an action against an individual of that studio. Personal assets can't be touched should the business go sour or if your partner gets the firm into hot water.

A corporation is much like a person in the eyes of the law — an entity separate from the owners. As a salaried shareholder, you are an employee of the corporation and must file legal papers and obtain a federal ID number.

The first stage of incorporation is known as a "C" corporation (and should you incorporate, you automatically become a "C corp."). Once incorporated, a business can then elect to become an "S" corporation. The "S corp." tax structure allows the corporation to be treated almost like a sole proprietorship, avoiding double taxation. Of course, your tax return would verify that the corporation's profits equal the sole proprietor's salary.

Examine the rituals involved in running a corporation. Study the tax laws, pension plans and savings options available. Consider the legal pros and cons. The decision must be based on your specific situation and as you do your homework, it will be readily apparent that expert legal and financial guidance will be needed.

Incorporation is a legal procedure requiring an attorney — your accountant cannot incorporate. But visit your accountant before you visit a lawyer. A lawyer is going to ask questions about taxes and accounting. Why do you want to incorporate? Do you have a federal ID number? Unless you see your accountant to secure those facts and figures, you may not have the answers for your attorney.

If you think that incorporation is the way to go, then double-check with your attorney to see if he or she agrees. In fact, if you are a graphic designer with minor assets, your lawyer may not recommend this — there simply may be no need for such protection. And yes, you can file papers of incorporation yourself, but you'll probably find the attorney's fee will be money well spent (usually $200 to $500).

As a last thought, grow into a corporation, don't rush into it.

Partnership Pitfalls

Do you need a partner? Do you want a partner? Let's discuss this by first offering a simple definition. A partnership is two or more people getting together and combining their assets and talents to form a business enterprise. Partners may offer numerous benefits, such as:

- Capital;
- Business acumen or creative prowess;
- An established clientele;
- Moral support;
- Fresh ideas;
- In-house feedback;
- Complementary skills.

A partnership can be a simple form of business. All you need is a handshake — you don't even have to have a formal written arrangement — and you can be partners. Thus, dissolution of a partnership is relatively easy, but notice I did not say it was painless. A business advisor may steer you away from such a venture. The problem is that a partnership has unlimited liability. So does a sole proprietorship, but many designers will tell you that a sole proprietor works to preserve his or her own best interests. With a partnership, there's another individual ostensibly acting as part of the team. Sadly for many failed partnerships, this teamwork was pure illusion.

A partnership could be equated to a working friendship (and we all know the joys and pitfalls of close friendships). Perhaps a more appropriate metaphor is to compare a partnership to a marriage; just like your spouse, you'd better know your business partner. Married life can be pain and/or pleasure. Divorce is invariably traumatic and devastating. So goes a partnership. Writing in *HOW* magazine, Joyce Stewart recommends, "Never just 'become partners' with another designer without developing a formal business agreement for the partnership — that's like marrying a blind date before you've met!"

Be smart. Write a practical, detailed document that will govern the arrangement of a partnership and address these real issues:

- Organization (who, what, when, where, how);
- Goals and purpose;
- Assets and contributions;
- How you will share profits (and losses);
- How you will divide responsibilities;
- Accounting procedures;
- Specifications of legal and financial powers;
- Grievance procedures (dispute resolution, mediation and arbitration);
- Dissolution procedures because of sale of interest, business termination, withdrawal, death, or expulsion of a partner;
- Growth procedures.

While it seems an exercise in morbidity to discuss some of this in those heady first days of the firm, that's exactly the right time. Change is inevitable, so be prepared. If you are thinking about taking on a partner, I highly recommend *The Partnership Book* (Nolo Press), by Dennis Clifford and Ralph Warner.

Finding Vendors and Suppliers

No designer is an island, so to speak. No matter how electronic your operation, you're not going to be able to do a job completely in-house; you'll need to use outside help at some point. Evaluate your needs and where to find that support team (copywriters, editors, printers, repro houses, typesetters, service bureaus, photographers, art supply stores, calligraphers, illustrators, retouchers, etc.). What contacts do you have already? How do you find vendors if you don't already know them?

Most support services are discovered through some rather basic sources: fingering through the Yellow Pages; recommendations from, or networking with, friends, family or other professionals; or by way of support services' promotions or advertising. Employ these traditional avenues to locate the crew you require. When you've located some supply sources, organize yourself by making a list and categorizing it into the following areas:

- **Studio help:** Includes freelancers, part-timers and clerical help — individuals who can help pick up the slack when you have more than you can handle.
- **Professional help:** Includes photographers, retouchers, illustrators, copywriters — other creative

Look for someone who complements your work style while filling in some gaps you might be lacking. Are you a specialist? Then look for a generalist. If you're the creative type, an ideal partner might also be creative, but have some business and sales skills. Look for someone with qualities you don't possess.

Valerie Ritter Paley, Ritter & Ritter, Inc.

professionals who supplement your capabilities by providing special talents.

- **Production services:** Includes all pre-press capabilities—service bureaus, stat houses, typesetting facilities, strippers and color separators.
- **Printers:** Include a range—from quick-print shops to book and catalog printers. You never know when you will need a company that specializes in embossing or a screen printer for a specialty job. Keep a record of what each printer does best and note the equipment available.

Set up a resource file for the above categories that includes information on each of the supply sources you are currently using or would like to consider for the future. You'll want to have alternatives and plenty of sources to choose from when trying to obtain the best price for a particular service. Use your files to keep track of quotes you've received from each of your current and potential suppliers. Generally, the word on the street will lead you to the service bureau or type house with the best deal, but printers may be another story. Sometimes they will lowball with the first job to get your business, and once they've proven themselves, will jack their prices up to the level of their competition. When you receive a promotion from a new supplier, throw it in the appropriate category as a fact sheet on that particular supplier.

Step 3: Will Your Plan Work?

Are your plans practical? Is your business truly viable? No matter what you want to do, you aren't going to work 12 hours a day, seven days a week—at least not without going crazy or getting sick. If it takes that kind of effort, your plans aren't realistic. If you can't write good ad copy now, you won't magically be able to when you're on your own, and so on. Your time is valuable, so examine your goals in the light of your knowledge, talents, strengths and weaknesses. Be blushingly honest with yourself. Your business will depend on an accurate assessment of what you want and your capability to accomplish that mission.

And How Will You Survive Tough Times?

Should business go sour, can you borrow money, live with family, sell your car, have a studio garage sale, or cut back on personal and/or business expenses? Could you freelance in someone else's agency, department or studio for a while? Share studio space or rent a portion of your space to someone else? Market another capability (like shooting stats for other designers/studios, etc.)? Rent out computer time to other designers or writers? Do typesetting for other designers/writers? Start a résumé service? Start a custom greetings/stationery shop? Write and design custom love/hate/complaint letters ("Two Macs—no waiting! No emotion too small!")? Ideally, you won't have to learn the dubious magic of the phrase, "Do you want fries with that?" However, in all seriousness, you might have to think of other options to support yourself if your business goes through a dry spell.

Step 4: Develop a Business Plan

Whether it be short and sweet or the size of *War and Peace*, an effective business plan must clearly detail your particular venture. Your business plan will help you to determine your future success by defining your goals, analyzing the competition and determining your risks. Your business plan says who you are, how you got here and where you're going. It is a personal, professional and financial yardstick that gives you a place to start, keeps you on track and helps you grow.

Because designers often start as a one- or two-person operation, they often start without a business plan. Writing a plan seems to be another formidable part of that bugbear called "business." All you need to start is a drawing board, some talented hands and a good printer at your disposal, right? Wrong. When the cash stops trickling in, when you're getting no response from your latest mailing, when it's your time in court after not being able to pay your printer, then you'll wish that you had planned more carefully.

A business plan won't solve all your problems, but it will give you a clear idea of what your problems might be and how you can prevent them from happening.

The Where, Why, How, When, Who and What

Your business plan is a personal statement of your goals. It can vary from a short summary to a full-blown document filled with marketing and financial projections. The length is up to you, but every business plan has six essential elements: where, why, how, when, who and what.

Where the business is to be located can be determined by its purpose, the competition, and its overall opportunities for success.

Why the business will succeed is determined by identifying your potential clients and why you have an advantage over your competition.

How describes the company's resources and its ability to carry out the plan.

When is indicated by milestones measured in profits, billings, number of clients, number of employees and so forth.

Who defines each person's specific responsibilities for accomplishing the goals of the business.

Wow, What I Did Wrong!

Your business will fail when (or if) you can't generate income. It will fail if you are not competitive in your pricing or if you do not provide quality service. Your business will fail if you are not aggressive enough when marketing your services or product. There are those individuals who are just not cut out to be businesspeople. Some folks go into business and live to mutter this about it: "Wow, what I did wrong!" I checked with other designers and businesspeople and came up with a top 20 list of complaints, excuses and famous last words:

1. I don't need an accountant/bookkeeper!
2. I shouldn't have rushed into this.
3. I had no financial cushion to fall back on.
4. Poor cash flow.
5. I picked a bad partner.
6. Getting a loan is going to be a piece of cake.
7. I didn't get enough funding.
8. I was underqualified.
9. I was overqualified.
10. Unrealistic? Me?
11. I got too big too fast.
12. I stayed small too long.
13. I suffered from promotional "underkill."
14. There was too much competition.
15. I was underpriced.
16. I was overpriced.
17. Legalities? What are those?
18. I don't have to hire anybody—I can do it all.
19. I really need all this fancy equipment and furniture.
20. Who needs a business plan?

What it costs is indicated by the cash flow projections.

You'll find more specific information in this book on how to pull together the details that will go into this plan. You will find out how to determine the most advantageous location for your business. You will learn how to identify prospective clients and how to convince them to use your services. You will find out how to make cost and income projections to help in the completion of this plan, but remember, change is constant. Revise your plan as needed to keep it timely and "do-able." Modify your operations accordingly.

Jilly Simons

Big Is Not Always Better

New York-born Jilly Simons grew up and worked in Johannesburg, South Africa, returning to America almost 15 years ago. Career moves eventually found her in Chicago, where she ultimately opened Concrete in 1987.

Concrete offers an intimate workspace. "I wanted my office to be very, very comfortable — and beautiful," Simons notes. "I created an environment I enjoy working in. And my intention is to keep the small, familiar atmosphere of the office," she adds. "Obviously, I want to increase the bottom line while maintaining the highest caliber of quality, but I don't want to grow a big office which could not afford the collective input of all its designers."

Simons spent many years working on staff before she went out on her own. "You get to a point in your career — you reach a certain stature — where you take charge anyway. You mature into it. I think for me it was a natural evolution.

"You want to make your own decisions or you don't want to be under somebody else's thumb," she says. "If you require any sort of autonomy, you automatically start going in that direction. And for years, I usually operated fairly autonomously within an organization.

"You're given particular responsibilities. I was dealing with clients directly. I inherited clients for one reason or another and developed new ones. I started handling estimating and billing or would work with the various account people developing budgets and marketing plans.

"A lot of designers just stumble around with this. Often they are not interested in planning or budgets, but I found the business end of things to be rather creative. I was always somewhat attracted to it. If your goal (at some point) is to run your own show, the best place to learn the ropes is within the arena of another organization, working with smart people and learning from them."

How do you know when you're ready for your own business? Says Simons, "That's a curious thing. I think you know when you're ready for a certain independence. For years I'd been in an extremely secure position but found myself

needing and wanting the freedom to make my own decisions without interference.

"What happened was that I went into a partnership, which was a good stepping-stone for me. I had the freedom, but still wasn't getting the autonomy that I wanted. There were other differences and we eventually went our own ways. That's when Concrete opened."

Was it tough breaking out of this situation? "I had insisted on a very formal partnership agreement, having learned from others who had wished they'd gone into partnerships with just such a contract. This allowed us a platform to separate from, which was very important. I'm pleased we did it — spent the money, suffered the headaches and hassles — prior to becoming a team. The split was fairly amicable. When you're separating monies, it's never pleasant, but we wrapped it up pretty well."

Best of all, Simons was now free to follow her head and heart. "I had this dream of a nice, small office that was very 'mean and lean.' It wasn't until well into my first quarter that I realized it could really work — that I did have a certain amount of business, and the studio could function the way I'd originally envisioned.

"I wrote a somewhat unofficial business plan — but for something as small and uncomplicated as

Concrete, I don't think you really need to write a business plan. It was basically just a balance sheet for me to work against (I work far too intuitively to do a formal strategic document). I need to know what my overheads are, what my expenses are, what's coming in and what's going out—quite basic.''

Run as a tight but congenial ship, Concrete is proof positive that a small creative studio can make it in the big, bad world of design. ''My goals have not changed, but my courage has increased,'' Simons will tell you. ''I set out to do good work and earn a living, not to get rich—although it would be delightful if that comes along. I hired dedicated people; we strive to serve our clients to the best of our abilities. And by keeping the margin for waste narrow, we can take on smaller, more daring and creative projects.

''In order to keep the overhead low, I can't take on expensive or very mature designers, so there is a natural attrition that will eventually have to happen. Once I've invested in somebody, I'd love them to stick around; but it's also up to them at that point. I've been pretty lucky. People do seem to enjoy working here.''

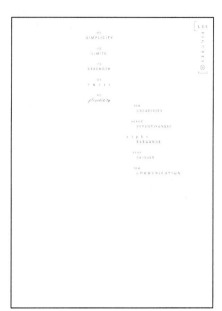

This unorthodox self-promotional brochure for Concrete has not only won awards but brought in many new clients for the firm.

Joel Fuller

Goals and Growth

At Pinkhaus, in Miami, Florida, creative director Joel Fuller and general manager Patrick Fiorentino disagree on the issue of growth. Fiorentino feels that operations on a large scope have an edge — that the bigger design businesses crackle

with the creative energies, personnel and resources necessary to turn out quality design. "From my standpoint," he says, "big is better because it affords us the infrastructure to produce better work."

To Fuller, "Big is not better. Often quality suffers with growth. But really, it's all relative — what is 'big'? Is big one [person]? A staff of five, or 10? Some folks consider Pinkhaus to be a big design firm [a staff of 15], but I don't."

"There are so many pieces to the puzzle," Fiorentino says. "It's all

very much an individual thing. We like this size because we enjoy the interaction. If you're happier as a sole proprietor working out of your garage, that's exactly what you should do."

Pinkhaus, which bills yearly in the seven-figure range, certainly started out small. Fuller had enjoyed a varied career up and down the East Coast, migrating between design studios and advertising agencies. In the belief that he could do better for himself, and for other designers, he founded Pinkhaus in April, 1985.

Leaving the comfort of a full-time job (along with designer and third partner Mark Cantor) was a leap of faith for Fuller. But he had a vision — Fuller dreamed of an open working environment where talented designers functioned as a powerful creative unit. "The philosophy is to bring people in, give them a stimulating atmosphere to do great design, pay them well, leave them alone and let them work. Challenge your people and they will grow. And as they grow, so grows the business," Fuller observes.

"To have one person's name on the door is rather like ridiculing that wisdom, so let's go with something else and make that name — make 'Pinkhaus' — become more than any one person."

Pinkhaus, which started up in

Fuller's condo, was originally "completely debt financed," as Fiorentino remembers. Initial business came from referrals and cold calls, capital from personal loans.

While there was no business plan, Fuller nevertheless had a goal-oriented approach. At an earlier job, Fuller received a valuable insight from a seasoned veteran. "The gentleman asked me what I wanted out of this business. I hadn't really thought about it and I replied, 'To do good work.' He said, 'No, what do you want materially? Write it down. Do you want a wife, a kid, a house, a boat, car, plane? Do you want to travel? Just write down what you want.'

"I wrote it all down," says Fuller, "and I went back to him and he said, 'Now put a dollar figure beside each one of those things.' I had never done this before. We added it all up and he said, 'There's no way you can have all of this without owning your own business.' "

Fuller says it had a lasting impact on his life. "What he did was make me assess my goals. From that point on, I couldn't comfortably work for anybody else. Every year I continue to rewrite those goals." Fuller says he asks himself questions like: What did I accomplish this year? What do I want to accomplish this year?

And for Pinkhaus, growth was a

predetermined goal. With additional business came the need for additional staff and Fuller's interactive group concept began to become a reality. "You're only as good as the people you hire and work with," he says. "When we first started, Mark and I knew we were weak on the business side. I didn't want to do it, so we brought Patrick in."

"We also saw we were really weak in production," notes Fuller. "The designers were trying to cover press production and take care of clients simultaneously. We ended up out of the office half the time [making press checks]. So we hired the finest production person we could find. If you're out there saying you can deliver the best product, you're not going to be able to deliver it unless you have the personnel. Talk is cheap — you have to be able to back it up."

And the folks at Pinkhaus mean what they say. Creativity and quality flourish against a comfortable, stimulating and high-energy backdrop. And while billings spiral upward annually, the partners apprise newcomers to a hard fact of business life. "You don't make money your first year," says Fiorentino. "Or your second or third year," adds Fuller. "When I first started the business, I thought I could make a profit in three years," he says. "Everybody told me it takes five to seven years, and they were right."

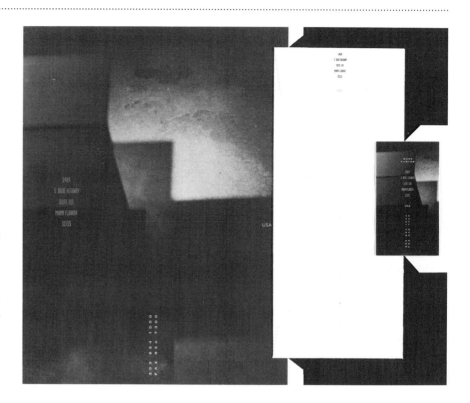

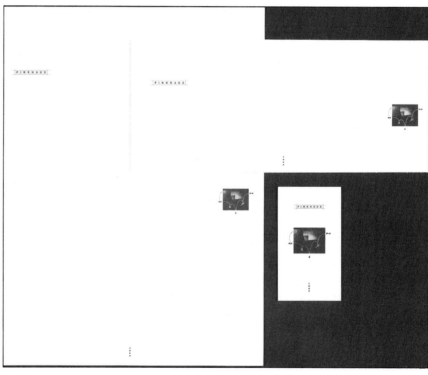

On April 1, 1992, Pinkhaus Design Corporation celebrated the completion of their seventh year in business. Their stationery no longer reflected where they were — nor where they wanted to be in the future. The fresh, exciting look of this new logo and letterhead system reflects Pinkhaus's new direction.

Arthur Ritter

The Perfect Partner

"Basically, I'm a creative person, and I wanted to see if I could function independently," says Arthur Ritter when asked why he started his own business in 1968. "I was spending more and more time on administrative duties with a large company and began looking at that at length. I realized that my training in administration wasn't strong, and I couldn't really go too far within this corporate structure with that kind of background.

"I had won some awards over a period of time. My outside assign-

ments started to increase. My freelance work was paying me almost as much as my full-time salary! *Newsweek* magazine and I made an arrangement for me to work on a freelance basis, contractually — that in itself paid for a good percentage of what I had been making on staff.

Ritter was fortunate to have *Newsweek* and other clients in place before he went out. "But the big problem," he says, "was setting up business structures — the account-

ing, how to bill, whether it would be a proprietorship or a corporation, keeping track of records and a variety of things."

Once he went into business on his own, Ritter's salary jumped so dramatically he was immediately audited. "This threw me into a kind of panic because I didn't realize that I had to keep such tight records of all my expenses — subway fares, bus fares and those kinds of things. That took the fun out of it for awhile. Keeping up creatively with the volume of work was also a hassle. I didn't realize how hard it is to work for oneself as compared to working on staff for someone else.

"You don't just walk out at five o'clock — it's the number of hours and the intense amount of labor that goes into the work. You're also proving yourself every time you're out. It's a cliché comment, but you're only as good as your last job."

When Ritter started Arthur Ritter, Inc. he initially set up at home, but then rented an apartment in the same building. The additional space also facilitated the hiring of freelance help — one full-time mechanical artist paid by the hour and another freelancer who worked and was paid by the project. "It was much more convenient to have the business in a different setting. I had basic equipment and some

savings. We sent out for stats but acquired a photostat machine later on. The biggest expenses were more than likely the photocopier and the rent.

"My basic goal was to see if I really enjoyed working for myself in that first year of business — to see if I could really survive creatively and independently," Ritter explains. As a result he didn't think it necessary to write a business plan. "We thought we would start out and see how far it would go, then decide whether or not to expand."

Ritter feels that survival as an independent businessperson depends a lot on the individual. "Do they have the talent? Do they want to spend long, long hours working? Is it worthwhile to invest the time and energy?" he asks. "You might make more money, as opposed to working on staff, but you develop a lot of gray hair working for yourself."

A cornerstone of Ritter's support has been his daughter, Valerie Ritter Paley. Paley joined the firm in 1983, but reminisces that she has been working with her father since "I was knee-high to a drawing board. We have been partners officially since 1988, when we renamed the company he founded Ritter & Ritter, Inc."

It comes as no surprise to many that this father and daughter team manages to work together so harmoniously. "Our partnership is successful because we complement each other's strong and weak points," says Paley. "We get along by being extremely professional about our relationship during work hours — trying to reserve personal asides or chitchat for later."

Paley believes that a good partnership in any business relies heavily on the personalities of the partners and their responsibilities. "At the core, partnerships should make a business run more smoothly, not be a hindrance," she says. "And if personalities are at odds, the latter can be the more likely.

"The main advantage is that of pooled resources, in terms of talent, time and finances. Of course, this also means that you might sink as well as swim together. Look for someone that complements your work style, while filling in some gaps you might be lacking. Are you a specialist? Then look for a generalist. If you're the creative type, an ideal partner might also be creative, but have some business and sales skills. Look for someone with qualities you don't possess."

While their work is collectively distinctive, the partners possess different areas of design expertise. "Arthur is much more strong with type than I am," says Paley, "and therefore handles covers, logos and newsletters more effectively. My forte is in more subtle, corporate communications as well as catalogs and annual reports that require organization and broader vision."

These partners also complement each other administratively. "Arthur is a super salesman, whereas I have a head for numbers and administrative work," says Paley. "While some of our clients prefer Arthur's style, others are more comfortable working with me."

Ritter sums it up by saying, "Merely possessing design talent doesn't necessarily mean you will have a successful business. So much depends on how you structure your firm, how well you plan and budget, and how effectively you reach out for new work."

By combining professional strengths with a team approach, the Ritters have shown that good design and sound business can indeed be a family tradition.

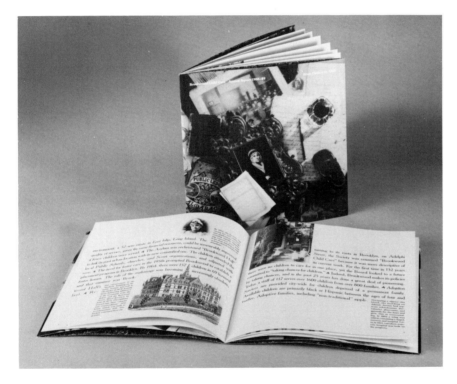

Since they began working together in 1986, Arthur Ritter and Valerie Ritter Paley have been doing award-winning design that gets results for their clients. These samples of their work — the 1986 annual report for Brookwood Child Care and these 1991 booklets for the Museum of Television and Radio — show how that tradition continues.

CHAPTER 3

SETTING UP SHOP

If you've always worked for someone else or are just getting out of school, you've probably never had to think about what equipment and supplies a studio needs. One of the joys of having your own studio is that now you can have exactly what you want — if you can afford it.

Before you run out and rent fancy office space and buy expensive furniture and equipment, you should determine what you'll need and why. Your first decision will be choosing where you want to work — at home or in a studio away from home — and what you must have to get your work done, possibly including a computer system (a big investment). Then you can start to plan for your own opening day in the space that's right for you.

Step 1: Decide Where You'll Work

You need a place to work. In theory, that can be anywhere you can get the work done. But in practice, your studio space must provide a professional atmosphere (especially for meeting clients). It must be an affordable place where you can concentrate and have enough room to do the job well.

Many designers feel they must have a fancy address in order to succeed, but that's simply not true. Although a ritzy-sounding address may attract certain clients, a prestigious address is not synonymous with premier design. However,

working in a clean, safe neighborhood will obviously help your credibility. You certainly don't want to set up shop in the heart of the high-crime district or in the middle of a heavily polluted industrial zone.

Your studio's location must also be practical. Consider proximity and access to clients, vendors and suppliers (and be sure your studio is within range of those suppliers who deliver). You want to be close enough to your clients so you can easily visit them and vice versa. You should be able to pick up supplies or drop off a job without having to drive long distances.

Working at Home or Away From Home

Some designers caution against the home studio, citing the major distractions of home, family and neighborhood. Throw in the potential client attitude that anyone working out of the house is not a true professional and you have a big red flag. But a good proportion of the designers interviewed in this book at least began their businesses working out of their apartments or houses. And the designers I interviewed who still have home studios wouldn't have it any other way.

Work at Home: Pros and Cons

Pros

- You don't have to pay for office space.

- You won't have extra utility and phone line costs.
- A home office is tax deductible (for example: a one-room studio in a five-room house garners you a 20 percent deduction off mortgage and utility costs).
- You can take care of business and chores.
- You can save on child care.
- You don't have to get dressed up each day.
- You can easily schedule work to suit your convenience.
- You save time and gas money by not commuting from home to work.

Cons

- You can't leave the office behind.
- Family and friends can interrupt a lot.
- You'll appear less professional.
- You can get distracted by housework and family responsibilities.
- You can spend too much time goofing off.
- Your workspace is inconvenient.
- Your work interferes with your personal life.
- Your personal life interferes with your work.

There are, of course, ways around the negatives if working at home is important to you. Don't try to set up a studio in the center of a bustling household. You must have privacy in which to work and a way to protect jobs in progress.

You need a door you can close on the design world as well as the living room. To appear your most professional, you can always meet clients at their offices (they'll probably love you for that) or have a separate door to the studio portion of your home. Or perhaps you can simply explain, "I hope you don't mind, but the studio's at the house. Be prepared for a warm, fuzzy and thrilling experience . . . no extra charge!"

Current technology and services have made the home office far more accessible than ever before. Indeed, computers and modems, fax machines and express mail couriers have transformed local studios, and cottage industries in general, into viable national (if not international) concerns.

A small but key concern will be swer your business phone—or the phone if you have only one line—during business hours. But can you afford two lines?

You may consider two phone lines a decided benefit if you fax frequently, dedicating one line exclusively to your fax. But you needn't have two lines to accommodate a fax. Most fax machines are now able to decipher between a fax and a voice message and route a signal to the proper destination (voice messages to the telephone, fax signals to the fax). If you decide your volume of calls and faxing only warrants one line, consider Call Waiting to inform you of incoming calls while you're engaged in a conversation. You never want to take a chance on missing an important call because the other party is turned away by a busy signal.

adequate space and wiring for your equipment? Can you maintain regular office hours at the house? How well will you be able to deter interruptions?

Working Away From Home: Pros and Cons

Pros

- You have a fixed center of business and communications.
- You provide a professional atmosphere (for you and your clients).
- Your environment is conducive to work (and reasonably free from the disturbances of family obligations).
- You project a professional image.
- Your work and personal lives are separate.
- You have better accessibility to vendors and delivery service if the location is in a commercially zoned area.

Cons

- It's more expensive—you're paying rent twice and shelling out extra bucks for utilities and furniture.
- You may need child care; you may miss your kids and the interaction with your spouse.
- You may not be able to dress casually or as comfortably as you prefer.
- Your workspace may not be in your location of choice.

I highly recommend starting at home—if you have the space and can isolate the studio. I have a child, and working at home has allowed me to be there and work in a wonderful, comfortable space. My clients think it's great!

Alyn Shannon, Shannon Designs

the business phone/controlling phone dilemma—the number of telephone lines you will need to maintain business communications (and that all-important professional atmosphere). Obviously, your three-year-old shouldn't an-

And don't forget the good ol' answering machine for fielding calls when you're not around or able to answer the phone.

Finally, consider other core issues when evaluating the home studio: Does your home provide

Ritter & Ritter, Inc.'s studio makes the most of its small area in Arthur Ritter's apartment.

- Time will be spent commuting between your home and studio.
- You may not have as much flexibility to work when the mood strikes you or at odd hours.

Whether you find the ideal office or simply know your home is just perfect, look at your potential studio and ask some critical questions: Are the space and facilities really right for your purposes? How's the storage? What about plumbing and sanitary facilities? How's the ventilation? How will you handle cleanup and waste removal? Do you have plenty of daylight, interior lighting and wiring? Is there parking? What's the traffic like at your location? Is the physical property easily accessible from the street? Is the studio easily accessible by standard modes of transportation? Is there adequate security?

You may want to consider a studio that, as real estate agents optimistically say, "needs some work." These work spaces, due to neglect or location, are in sub-par condition. If your future office is the proverbial "handyman's special," evaluate how much time, energy and resources will be spent to get the place safely up to code and to suit your needs. If your goal is to get

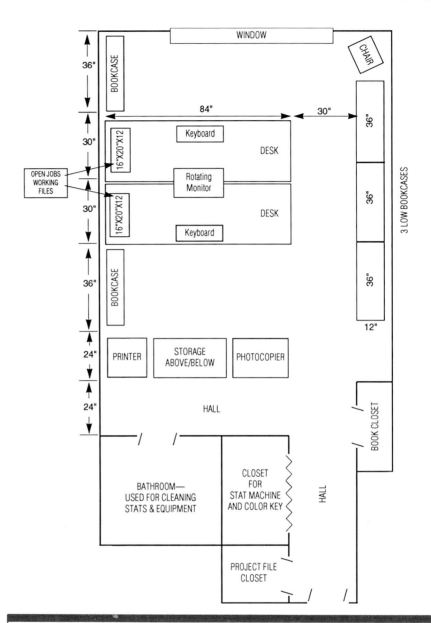

Available Space

Arthur Ritter and Valerie Ritter Paley of Ritter & Ritter, Inc., work out of a 10-by-16-foot room in Arthur's two-bedroom apartment. Valerie credits Arthur's ingenuity for getting the most out of their limited space. "We actually have fit quite comfortably in the studio area a Mac II (the monitor's on a swivel with two keyboards so we can both use it), a modem, an Imagewriter LQ printer, a photocopying machine, a stat camera and developing unit, a color key machine and a waxer, as well as two large desks, supplies such as pads and boards, an extensive library of design reference books and current client files."

your business quickly up to speed, I would discourage you from going this route. There's only so much of you to go around, and I believe your energies should be directed to becoming a freelance designer, not Joe Contractor.

You may want to look into leasing or buying a condo, renting part of an office suite, or sharing space with another designer or a photographer (or an even larger group). There are benefits in mutual space: a common receptionist and conference room, sharing large equipment, splitting expenses and overhead, and there's valuable camaraderie, in-house feedback, and a ready-made support system.

The Lease
You've found this great loft space north of Rialto, just off the Dakota district—very close to Joanne's Art Supply. Good light, lots of room. Absolutely right for the office. The landlord smiles and says, "Just sign on the dotted line, Ms. Designer. Don't worry about all that stuff down there. Pay no attention to that little paragraph set in tiny type. Oh, that clause? It's nothing,

nothing at all."

Hold on. Study your entire lease very carefully. Remember that the lease was prepared for the landlord, so it's written with his needs, not yours, in mind. A lease is, however, subject to negotiation.

Even though this office is to die for, show the lease to your lawyer before you sign it. Examine the lease together. Be sure you truly understand the terms. Can these terms somehow change during the course of your lease? Can the landlord legally cancel your lease? How

and why? Can you legally break the lease? How, when and why? Here's a checklist of points you should be aware of in addition to the rent.

- Length of the lease (shorter is better);
- When and how the deposit may be forfeited;
- Restrictions on how you may use the space;
- Zoning requirements;
- Option to continue or renew the lease;
- Cost for continuing or renewing the lease;

Adela Ward Batin's office occupies an 800 square foot space that she designed for maximum efficiency and comfort. Starting from a tiny studio in her home, she now has state-of-the-art typesetting equipment, plenty of working surfaces and flat files, a conference room, a reception area, her private office—and a gorgeous view of the Alaska mountain range.

I wanted to get away from the studio once in a while so, even though it was expensive, I set up in an office.

Rick Tharp, Tharp Did It

- Whether you can sublet or assign the lease;
- Who is responsible for cleaning and repairs;
- Who is responsible for what utilities;
- Who is responsible for maintenance;
- Whether the landlord has the right to move tenants.

I converted a detached one-car garage into an office. Cold in winter, but great most of the year. I wanted to keep costs to a minimum as well as have the convenience of working out of my home. My mother thinks I started freelancing so I could spend more time with my cat. (Only partly true.)

Vicki Vandeventer, Vandeventer Graphic Design

Step 2: Decide Whether You'll Use a Computer

Many designers have already found the computer to be a fast, powerful and versatile design tool. From roughing out concepts and visualizing to creating actual illustrations, as well as for typesetting and preparing comps, mechanicals or finished art, computers are invaluable to these artists and designers. Computers are also used to streamline the business end of design. It's safe to say that you may want to buy a computer for tracking expenses and time, billing, record-keeping, and project storage (page

layouts, type and logos can all be stored on disk). Or you may never purchase a computer at all. In this day and age that might sound positively blasphemous to the computer convert, but I know people who still use pencil, paper, markers and press type for everything from thumbnails to printed piece and refuse to abandon them.

A needs assessment can be very helpful in determining whether or not you should get a computer. Consider what you want the system to do, your available resources (both skill and money), and the time frame available for making your decision and implementing your system. Time is important. A

common error is to wait for the "latest and the greatest" and never get started. Don't make excuses—if you decide to get a computer, go ahead and jump in!

Whether or not you should take the plunge at all is a personal decision, and should be based on your assessment of your needs, personality and budget. I myself can't get along without that little box parked prominently on the desk in my study. I thought my Mac would just be a graphics solution, but it has also become a business lifesaver. It's always fun and exciting to work at the computer. Easy to learn, yet a most challenging and interesting work device, the Macintosh provides a happy marriage of process and product that's extremely satisfying. Although my Mac can never replace the rush I get from the flow of watercolors or the scratch of a pen on good paper, it's a high-powered instrument that adds a lot to my toolbox.

I can't tell you whether getting a computer will be as helpful for you

I shopped smart in terms of finding a space to keep my overhead low. I wanted to enjoy the pleasure of having a nice atmosphere around me without the load of high rent.

Jilly Simons, Concrete

as it has been for me. I can, however, give you some background about what systems can contribute to your creativity and business. We'll also discuss what to look for and what to ask when window-shopping and then buying (or leasing) a computer. (First, though, a word of caution: As computer technology roars by the consumer like a rocket, prices as well as hardware and software change almost monthly and will most likely have changed between the time of this writing and the time you read this. Use this info as a shopping aid, not as a definitive buyer's guide.)

Why/Why Not Buy a Computer

Yes, I'll Take It!

- To gain greater control of the design and production processes;
- To make corrections and client changes faster and cheaper;
- To see how "real" type and copy look on the page instantly;
- To explore more variations in less time;
- To get more done in less time;
- To cut time and production costs;
- To reduce paperwork and streamline procedures;
- To keep up with or get ahead of your competition.

No, I Won't!

- Hardware and software cost too much;
- Technology keeps changing

("I'll wait");
- Don't want to be a typesetter or separator;
- Don't know much about computing;
- Don't like computers;
- Unimpressed by computer designs/illustrations;
- Just don't need one;
- It's too hard to learn;
- Don't want to be left in the lurch if the system crashes.

What System Is Right for You?

I'm not beating the drum for either the Macintosh or IBM and its compatibles (MS DOS-based systems are often called "PCs"). What's best? Is it simply a matter of right brain versus left? Will an icon-based operating system actually be faster and easier to use than a keyboard-based one? Are MS DOS systems cheaper and more powerful than Macs? It depends on how you're most comfortable working and what you want to do.

Over time, the Mac and the PC have moved closer to each other. Powerful word processing and business-related software (plus beefier hardware) are now available for the Mac. New operating systems and new or redesigned software for the PC emphasizes ease of use, icon-based interfaces and sparkling graphics. There are still distinctions as of this writing, but those are blurring. It all comes down to a question — and the accurate evaluation — of your situation,

preferences, time frame for growth, and available funds.

All the designers interviewed for this book who use computers employ a Macintosh as a design, production and business tool. The Mac appears to be the computer of choice for designers, so there's an extensive support network for those just beginning or testing the waters. The Mac's high-resolution visuals, icon-based interface, consistency of command sets for all software (for instance, Command-S is "Save File" in every program), and the availability of design- and illustration-related software have made it the darling of the design world.

On the other hand, the lawyers, accountants and tax specialists I talked to employ IBM computers or compatibles. The PC crunches numbers, juggles data, and does word processing and text editing skillfully. It's a seasoned veteran with plenty of software available. Lump in speed, power, proven technology and price, and PCs have the edge over the Mac as a general business machine.

As of this writing, there is a ground swell of enthusiasm (and much hype) surrounding what some label the "True Designer's Machine": Steve Jobs' NeXT computer. The NeXT is an innovative and beautiful piece of equipment boasting power and features found on most wish lists. Of course, quality and performance do not come cheap, but computer prices drop over time. The second generation of NeXT computers are already more powerful, efficient, and less expensive than the original machine.

You may want to investigate the Amiga system from Commodore. These relatively inexpensive computers feature fine color and graphics capabilities and could be considered the entry into economical animation.

Then there's the other end: dedicated systems like the $100,000 Lightspeed. MACs and PCs are the multipurpose generalists of the computer world and are designed to be jacks of all trades, to handle a legion of computing tasks (word processing, accounting, graphics, games). Lightspeed and other dedicated systems (such as Quantel or Aurora) are built to do one thing—graphic design—with breathtaking speed, awesome power and amazing grace.

Software and What

But no matter how fancy the computer system, the most powerful machine remains humbled without the right software. As an artist and businessperson you will need a variety of applications to effectively run your complete studio: design software, word processing software for correspondence, a file-keeping database, accounting and/or bookkeeping programs, and organizational software for your office management.

When it comes to graphics software, it's a real buyer's market. A designer can pick and choose from many possible options. There are programs for basic design, page layout and typography; there are drawing, color rendering and paint programs to do everything from sketches to final art; and also 3-D, animation packages and presentation programs. You'll find a variety of entry level, mid-range and high-end applications (determined by a combination of price, degree of difficulty and features). No matter where you are on the learning curve you should be able to find graphics software to meet your needs.

The same applies to word processing. Vendors' shelves boast a wide spectrum of software from slick to simple for your selection. The rich cornucopia of choices offer basic writing tools to advanced text manipulation.

What does the small design studio need in terms of business software? As mentioned earlier, electronic spreadsheets, databases, communications software and accounting packages can help a creative artist manage an efficient and organized business. Look into integrated (all-in-one) packages (such as Microsoft Works) or bundled software that combine the basic business applications—text, spreadsheet, database and telecommunications.

But will packaged software be right for you? Consultant and programmer Steve Ledingham, owner of Ideas Unlimited in Dayton, Ohio, says, "The computer shouldn't be telling you how you think. You should be telling the computer how you think. Work with a consultant or programmer. If you're looking for business or accounting software, consider having the software designed for you rather than trying to buy software that fits your particular situation. As your business grows, with a bit of training you could then customize and expand a starter package to meet other needs and do a whole lot more."

On the other hand, Mike Parsons, owner of Cottage Computer Systems, Inc., cautions that the cost of custom-built software may be prohibitive. Parsons correctly observes that, "There's an abundance of reasonably priced, extremely versatile software available today."

Indeed, specialized programs or general-purpose applications designed to handle most of your business chores can be found on the shelf. With a bit of research you can get great performance and good value. Ask other designers what programs they use and prefer. If you can't get to a store, you need go no further than the current computer magazines and catalogs. Window-shop a few magazines, read the reviews, or call the mail-order houses for recommendations. Remember, even a bit of information can go a long way; make an educated decision and purchase.

Whether you're buying graphics, business or word processing software, get plenty of input first. Your friends, user groups, and computer or desktop publishing magazines can tell you not only what's out there but what's hot and what's not. Compare features and prices before you buy, and always test drive the program first to make sure it does what you want it to do. Fool around with the program on a friend's computer. Take it for a spin at your local dealer. Buy from a mail-order business that offers a 30- to 60-day money-back guarantee and give the program a trial run.

Just Tell Me What You Want

All time expended assessing your needs before you buy a computer or software is time well spent. Here's a list of points to consider:
- Who will use it? Just you or you and your partner or staff?
- Why are you planning to buy? What specifically do you expect a computer to do for you? If you want to improve productivity or cut costs, how will a computer help you do that?
- What exactly will you use it for—bookkeeping, outputting type, creating illustrations, designing, page layout, word processing, etc.?
- What quality of output do you

Create Your Own Business Package

Steve Ledingham advocates a package that merges basic bookkeeping with a master address file and billing generator. "This can be done by means of a non-relational database—what's called a 'flat file.' The advantage of this flat file is that it can easily be customized by the user without approaching a consultant or programmer."

Ledingham isn't suggesting you get a complicated financial program. "A good quality flat file database in conjunction with a spreadsheet may meet your needs. Don't even call it a database; call this the information handler," he continued. "You'll want an information handler with automatic math functions—one that can track clients plus job times, then make

nice looking invoices. Extract the figures from your flat files, run the numbers through the electronic spreadsheet (to be sorted by category with dates, amounts and totals), print it out and present this to your accountant as a ledger sheet.

"At some point in the future, if and when needs dictate—and finances permit—look into a fully relational database for your growing business. A high-end information handler will perform sophisticated calculations and look-ups combined with a custom billing system, giving you complete accounting functions. This powerful software will let you do just about anything, but I urge designers not to overdo it in terms of what they really need."

---

need? High quality—1,250 dots per inch (dpi); mid-range—300 dpi; or low quality—72 dpi dot matrix printing? Do you need to output color? Create transparencies?
- Where will you do input and output? One workstation or more? Will you need to deliver material to a service bureau frequently and therefore need a modem? Will you be networking with other computers via disk translation (such as Appletalk or

Ethernet)?
- Will you need a scanner for working with existing photos, drawings and slides?
- When do you want to be partially or fully computerized?
- How much will it cost? What can you afford? Where will you get the money?
- How will your system be supported: Who will train you, help you solve problems (technical support), and fix your equipment when it's not working? If

you can afford the services of one, a consultant is an invaluable ally (see below for more on consultants). Don't underestimate the time and money involved in keeping your computer system up and running effectively.

Whatever (and wherever) you buy, consider working with a consultant. If you can afford one, it's to your definite advantage to have a consultant on tap. Find a people-oriented expert who knows the hardware and software and who will be there when you need support, training or advice. To locate a consultant talk to friends, check the phone book and then interview. You might also consult vendors or user groups, even though it's a slight conflict of interest. Vendors will naturally promote use of the hardware and software they sell. User groups—in the effort to promote computer literacy and autonomy—will steer you toward what they know and use.

You may be able to find a Value-Added Resaler (VAR), a person or dealership authorized to sell some particular equipment, who will act as your consultant. These may be either small stores such as Cottage Computers in Dayton, Ohio, or national chains such as Computerland. Look for an operation that emphasizes, as part of the sale, sustaining a relationship with the client *after* the purchase. This is the

best of all worlds—sales, service and support all in one. It's worth the search and possibly higher prices to find such a store.

Making the Buy

Evaluate what you want to do but don't overbuy. Mix and match speed, power, memory and storage with some flexibility—keep an eye on your future. Get plenty of memory and storage: at least 2 to 4 megabytes (MB) of Random Access Memory (RAM) and a 40 to 80MB hard drive. Purchase a monitor with a screen as large as you need but only invest in a color monitor if you truly need one.

Consider speed and power, too. The following numbers refer to the size of the computer's processor (the unit that does the actual work of the machine). On a PC, you'll need what's called an "80286, 80386 and 80486" machine. The "286" is entry level; the "386" and "486" are faster and more powerful but also more expensive. On the Mac, the coprocessor "6800" is entry level, while the "68020," "68030," and "68040" are the faster, more expensive versions.

It's a common complaint that the buyer can't keep up with technology. Hardware and software improve so dramatically and so fast that many users moan that a system becomes obsolete as soon as you unpack it. Because of this situation, specific information given at this

writing may well be ancient history by the time you read it. Therefore we must approach the market in general terms.

Currently a low-end Macintosh system, monochrome monitor, dot matrix printer and some software (entry-level word processors, paint and/or drawing programs and flat file databases) costs about $2,000. A medium-range system, running in the $3,000 to $4,500 neighborhood, might include a more powerful CPU (central processing unit), a moderately priced laser printer, larger monitor (a full- or two-page display), or perhaps a color monitor. (A good shopper can even add a modem and a scanner and still fall under the $8,000 mark.) A high-end system based on a state-of-the-art Mac, high quality laser printer, gray-scale or color monitor, and the peripherals already mentioned (for a medium-range system) would start at about $9,000.

Actual numbers will differ, but the scenario for an IBM-compatible or PC purchase will play the same—you pay more for extra and better equipment.

Where to start your shopping? Do your homework. Learn what available hardware and software meet your needs and budget. Talk with friends, buy a few periodicals, browse the stores, and check with other designers who use computers and software that interest you. Then seriously shop around. You can buy both software and hardware at a store, by mail order, from a VAR or through a consultant. Each of these outlets has its fans and critics. Unless you network, comparison shop, research and read (including the fine print), ask questions, weigh the pros and cons carefully, and know exactly what you want, you probably won't get a good deal anywhere. But this is true of buying a car, furniture or stove. The old caveats apply even more to our new high tech gear: buyer beware, buyer prepare.

While price is important, it's not the only consideration. A great bargain may not be the best computer for you. Inquire about the following before you buy:

- How long has the vendor/ dealer/VAR/consultant been in business? How accessible are customer service, repair and training centers? Can the vendor/dealer/VAR/consultant supply references from previous customers?

- What is the cost of the basic system components (versus your budget and in general)? What equipment is really included in that price?

- What are the system's requirements in terms of power, space, ventilation?

- What kinds of training and support are available? Do you get any free training? How much? How long does it take most users to learn this system?

- What kind and amount of software are available for and compatible with your hardware and at what prices?

- What add-ons are available?

- How are upgrades (customizing to create a bigger, better machine) and trade ups (swapping to acquire a bigger, better machine) handled?

- Get a sense of the top limits on what your hardware and software can handle (number of users, programs and projects).

- Can you network your system and software easily?

- What are the policies on returns? What is the system's or software's record for reliability? Can it be serviced locally or will it have to go back to the manufacturer? Are service contracts available and how much will they cost?

Comparison Pricing

Getting the lowest possible price shouldn't be your sole prerequisite for buying a certain computer at a particular store, but you should shop around. For smart and efficient shopping, organize your information by adapting the buyer's guides on page 40; this will help you pinpoint the best deal and where to get it. Computer consultant Steve Ledingham of Ideas Unlimited uses these guides to make recommendations to his clients. It's easy. Vendor information goes on top. Next, info on each component is gathered over the phone, in person, or from classified ads and

The Leasing Alternative

Should you lease your equipment instead of buying it outright? That depends on your financial and tax situation. There are advantages and disadvantages to leasing. Leasing may give you lower monthly payments over a longer period of time than an outright purchase. You can buy your machine at the end of the lease (terms for this vary, but are generally about 10 percent of the total cost), renew the lease, or trade up to newer and better equipment. Because you may have to pay top dollar for a system, this can be a more expensive way to go, but many dealers include a service contract and access to some technical support as part of your lease (not all do, so be sure to read your lease carefully). Without a service contract, you'll be responsible for repairs. The cost of your lease is tax-deductible annually, which may be a better deal for you than taking the depreciation allowance from an outright purchase. If your accountant suggests leasing as an option, check it out.

store advertisements. Remember to research both new and used equipment (if available).

Step 3: Choose Your Supplies and Equipment

"Like a kid in a candy store" may accurately describe the designer at the art/office supply house, but it's important to choose only what you really need, can afford, and can fit into your space. A computer will eliminate some of your paste-up and technical drawing, but you'll still need traditional paste-up and drawing equipment. So you will have to realistically assess what supplies you'll need, their cost, and how much space to allot to your traditional equipment and computer supplies.

A list of supplies and equipment could go on and on. Some obvious wants and needs are:

Can't Start Without
- Drawing table or drawing board
- Worktable
- Light table or light box
- Storage: shelves, cubbyholes, boxes, etc.
- File holders or filing cabinets
- Chair(s)
- Lights and lamps
- Art and production supplies
- Office supplies
- Address file
- First aid kit

VENDOR NAME: _____	FOR Company Name: _____
Phone: _____	Phone: _____
Contact Person: _____	Contact Person: _____
Date of Contact: _____	Date of Contact: _____
Address: _____	Address: _____
City/State/ZIP: _____	City/State/ZIP: _____
Source: _____	

CPU			PRINTER			STORAGE		
Model	New	Used	Model	New	Used	Model	New	Used

KEYBOARD			APPROXIMATE TOTAL COST		
Model	New	Used	Item	Model	Amount
			CPU		
			Monitor		
			Keyboard		
			Card(s)		
			Drive(s)		
			Storage		
			Printer		
			Cables		
			Additional		
			Subtotal I		

MONITOR					
Model	New	Used	Setup		
			Consultation Fee		
			Subtotal II		
			Training		
			Technical Support		
			Subtotal III		
			Software		
			TOTAL		

This worksheet, based on guides Steve Ledingham of Ideas Unlimited uses, will help you comparison shop for the best deal on your computer set up. Fill out one sheet for each vendor you contact. Try to keep the components in the same order on each section so you don't end up accidentally comparing a high priced computer with a lot of memory with one that has a lower price because it has less memory.

- Typewriter or word processor if you don't have a computer
- Phone
- Answering machine
- Stationery
- Some promotional material
- Business cards and forms

Handy to Have
- Coat rack or closet
- Additional work surfaces
- Desk (real one makes bill-paying, etc. easier than working on the drawing board)
- Flat files or racks for storing

projects (storing project boards between rounds of changes is a hassle otherwise)
- Computer and software
- Photocopier with reduction/enlargement capabilities
- Guest chairs and table for meeting with clients
- Slide projection and/or viewing system
- Basic kitchen supplies, coffee maker
- Fax machine

Only If You Can Afford It
- Stat camera
- Multiline phone
- Intercom

I've been very careful to buy things only as I need them or when I find a terrific bargain. I paid next to nothing for my used stat camera — just happened to see an ad for it in the paper. Bought a used copier, too, from one of my clients. Another client paid for half of my fax machine when I needed it for one of their projects.

Vicki Vandeventer, Vandeventer Graphic Design

- Music system
- Video cassette recorder

New, Used or Leased

In my discussions with the designers in this book we identified what was jokingly referred to as "Designers' Disease": the craving to have only the newest and best of everything. (Is this malady exclusive to the design world? Certainly not, but let the plumbers complain about it in their own book.)

If you have the cash available (see page 51 on calculating and monitoring your cash flow), an outright purchase is cheaper. You own the furniture or equipment without the hassle of payments — and there are no interest charges. But will you be able to sell an obsolete piece of equipment (if you can't trade or upgrade it) or used furniture to recover part of your investment?

Is used equipment or furniture a good alternative? That's a big maybe. "Buyer beware" says it best. Cheap, previously owned equipment may look like a bargain, but do your homework and shop around before you say "yes." Definitely negotiate for a trial period, a repair warranty and terms for return. It's also wise to have the item thoroughly, professionally inspected before you buy.

Before you decide, get your accountant's advice, too. It sometimes makes more financial and tax sense to finance or even to lease big ticket items. A leasing company may decline to lease you some equipment if you haven't been in business a certain number of years (an indication of stability and ability to pay), unless there's a personal guarantee. Leasing has tax advantages — you can write off your entire payment — and does allow you to upgrade your equipment with a minimum of fuss. Often you'll have the option to buy at the end of the lease. Investigate interest rates carefully, especially when choosing between leasing and financing a purchase.

Step 4: Prepare for Opening Day

You'll need to gear up for that first day of business. The preconception that a designer just casually strolls into a new workspace and becomes a business is woefully wrong. But any dread of the work required — or planning involved — is also misguided.

To get a handle on what to do before your doors open, I've grouped items (and set up a table) sequentially to help you prepare for your big day. You'll find more information on these aspects of starting your studio in other chapters, so I'll only hit the highlights here. For example:

Five weeks to a month prior to opening, you should visit your accountant; work up your first promotion, business forms, cards and letterheads; acquire all permits and licenses; lay down the rent deposit and get the keys.

One month to three weeks before opening day, you should see your lawyer; create your business's sign or have it made; print the promo, the business forms and the identity.

Two weeks to opening, mail the promo; place your advertising; buy a phone (and fax) — and get your phone line(s) hooked up; hand over your deposit and have the utilities turned on; build shelving, etc.

One week to the big day finds you picking up your business forms and identity materials; installing the store sign; signing up for cleaning services, etc.

Adapt my form to suit your own needs. You will find that following this basic road map will get you down the path to opening day easily and efficiently. Of course, you also need to plan these expenses carefully so you don't end up over your head in debt before you even open. You don't want your gala opening to be followed immediately by your going out of business party. (For more on calculating and budgeting for your start-up costs, see page 49.)

CONCRETE

THE OFFICE OF JILLY SIMONS

OPENED ON

DECEMBER FIRST

NINETEEN HUNDRED AND

EIGHTY-SEVEN

633 SOUTH PLYMOUTH COURT

SUITE 208

CHICAGO. ILLINOIS 60605

312.427.3733

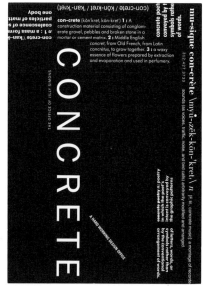

Jilly Simons sent this simple, classic announcement with its lively insert to let potential and former clients know that she had opened her own studio.

TASK	WEEKS BEFORE OPENING AND ANY CASH REQUIRED				OPEN	WEEKS AFTER OPENING AND ANY CASH REQUIRED			
	5-4	4-3	2	1	0	1	2	3	4
See lawyer									
See accountant									
Do initial ad									
Place ad									
Do/print promo									
Send promo									
Phone hook-up									
Get city permit									
Buy fax									
Utilities on and deposit									
Yellow Pages listing									
Rent deposit and get keys									
Sign made									
Sign installed									
Do card and letterhead									
Do business forms									
Print all									
Pick-up printing									
Refreshments for open house									
Sign up cleaning service									
Build shelves									
Cash Needed									

Use a chart like this to plan your grand opening. Place an *X* in the right column for each item or enter the costs for each in the appropriate space.

Peg Esposito

Working From Home Is Best

Peg Esposito has situated her recently incorporated company, Peg, Inc., in what she considers the best of all locations: her home.

A seasoned art director, Esposito sandwiched a prior stint of freelancing between years of full-time agency experience before starting her present business. With a track record both in and away from her Wisconsin residence, Esposito unabashedly extols the joys of working from the house. But it took two freelance attempts for Es-

posito to understand how and where to play the game. She worked as art director at a small agency for four years before initially going out on her own. "As a staff artist I was working more and more hours and making no more money. I figured the least that could happen if I freelanced was that I would earn more money for more hours worked. A great premise," she says, "until you run across a bad sheep client that won't pay."

So Esposito returned to another full-time advertising job for 2½ years. On her second attempt — and unlike her first — she was prepared for the realities of having her own business. She had savings that would cover her living expenses for several months, and she'd been moonlighting as a freelancer while working at the second agency, so she had three or four accounts lined up when she started. "I had a two-week slow spell that first year — which was horrendously nerve-wracking — and then my business went gangbusters."

After working both for herself and for someone else, Peg knew she was happiest on her own. "I am a solo agent at heart. I enjoy the freedoms of freelancing. It's risky going out on one's own. And there is a lot of work other than the creative process to be done. But the rewards are all yours. It is the freedom to work when and where you wish; the self-determination of being able to work with only those you want to work with; driving your job in the direction you want; the self-satisfaction of nurturing a business and watching it grow and mature."

Peg set up shop at home and loves it. "Most of the attraction in working out of my house comes from being able to work at the board in shorts and a T-shirt — no makeup, nylons or uncomfortable

shoes. That, and the option to work until 2:00 A.M., then drop directly into bed without having to travel from office to home." An admitted workaholic, Peg says, "I can stretch any job to fill all my time — especially if the alternative is housework. Where's the choice in 'Should I dust or design?'

"I hope always to work from my home. But over the years, I have found living space that has an office room somewhere so I can close the door. When I began freelancing (my studio) fit into a corner of my living room, which suddenly became 'work central.' This is fine, until it's time to entertain, then finding temporary places for those same piles of work becomes a job in itself. Plus, every time I wanted to relax in my living room, I was faced by an incomplete project. It started to take its toll."

Esposito reclaimed her personal space when she returned to a full-time job, and later still when she began freelancing the second time in this same apartment. Moving the office back home called for total reorganization (and once again losing that precious living area). This time, however, she had shelves that would close. "Hiding the studio in time for a date was a hassle, but not insurmountable.

"My husband and I eventually found a great two-bedroom place and my office finally had a room of its own," she continues. "It was amazing how different my job suddenly felt! I had a place to go to work and a place to relax. There was a defined space for projects, and there was an 'off-limits' space." Recently the couple have purchased a house in Wisconsin, which, of course has a room for Peg, Inc.

Esposito feels that having a home office is worth "all of the hassles of living with the mess, and I would do it all again. Having my own time schedule, being my own boss and being able to work comfortably supersede the need to have perfect work conditions." Being frank, she hopes never to locate the studio in her living room again, but asserts, "If faced with the choice of finding a 'real job' or working in the same area that I live, my vote goes to freelancing."

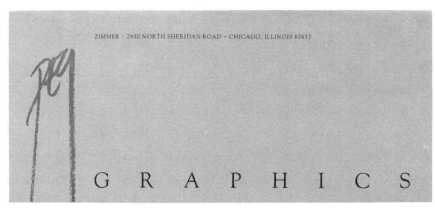

The evolution of Esposito's letterhead, as shown by these envelopes, has mirrored the evolution of her business. She started with a simple design and added new elements as her business grew (and she married and moved). The final letterhead for Peg, Inc. retains the casual "Peg" signature while adding a more formal block logo to the design.

Starting on a Shoestring

Alyn Shannon simply calls her business Shannon Designs. Her one-woman shop boasts nationally recognized graphics; it's a modest operation that stays small but does "big" work. How did the Minneapolis, Minnesota, designer establish her studio?

After four years as a paste-up artist for a small ad agency, Shannon went in-house to set up a graphics department for one of that agency's clients. Six years later she took her design and corporate communications experience and went on a contract basis with the same corporation. This allowed her to develop additional clients and maintain a source of income. But Shannon wanted more control. "I wanted to earn what I made in-house at this mid-size company, and then maintain steady income growth from there." Setting up an office at home, she discovered that establishing herself as a freelancer wasn't easy. "I worked harder than ever — managing all the jobs, doing everything myself. At the beginning you can never say 'no.' You don't turn any work down."

Shannon used her savings as seed money for her start-up. She started with a minimum of equipment and supplies — "A drawing table, art supplies, some drafting equipment. I did have an Arto-

graph and a small Apple computer I used for accounting. My biggest expense was remodeling my home to create studio space.

"In this day and age the computer has become an absolute necessity. When I set up my business in 1987, less cash was needed for just that reason. In 1993, Macintosh computers are not the exception — they're the rule! After installing my system two to three years ago, 100 percent of my jobs are now designed, typeset and keylined on the Mac. I then either modem or release SyQuest disks of my files directly to the printer." Shannon benefits from being linked with a Scitex system — no more traditional type and keylines.

"I think in today's graphics market you *have* to know how to design and produce on a Macintosh. I took some courses at my area Vo-Tech college, and then taught my-

self programs like FreeHand, Illustrator and Photoshop.

"I purchased a Mac IICX as my first design station. Over the years I have upgraded to a Quadra with a 200 meg hard drive, SyQuest and an optical drive to give my system enough memory to store large files. A lot of storage space is a necessity when you work with photos and art. I spent $20,000 for that initial system, but can earn that back quickly on type savings alone!

"The computer revolution has happened. Fortunately, I had the traditional production knowledge and design skills to apply to the new technology. I think that starting out today would be a lot different, but I'd do it again — I love working for myself. The Mac offers so much flexibility and capability; I earn more now than I ever thought possible (I also work harder); and best of all — there are no corporate politics."

Shannon's logo — a striking box made up of a bright blue triangle and a magenta triangle with a white triangle set inside it — attracts the viewer's eye to her business card.

Mike Quon

Realistic Dreams

Mike Quon attended UCLA in the early '70's, majoring in design and advertising. While still in school, Quon began working as a free-lancer. Following graduation, Quon accepted and soon departed from a full-time staff position as a graphic designer. Leafing through the phone book led him to discover a large food services corporation right in his neighborhood. He

cess to dash to New York in 1976 with "a little bit of money and a lot of big dreams." Although his L.A. business had been a success, Quon was attracted to the activity and challenge of "making it" in New York. "I called (and called on) people every day." Challenged by the pace and pulse of the city, Quon started his fledgling enterprise in a corner of a loft he found in Soho where he still lives today.

the business except for a 6-by-6-foot sleeping area. There was no separation of home and office; I would end up working 20 hour days — this takes a toll." Quon's ample loft, once his comfortable home, was now a small, cramped studio space.

Needing to expand, Quon heard about openings in a large factory building located on Broadway. The place was being divided into lots of 2,000 square feet, and the space was quickly attracting a lot of photographers, designers and art galleries. Since his business was booming and busting out of his current work environment, and he wanted to grow, in 1985, Quon took a 10-year lease on what he labels "the big move" out of his house.

Quon now feels he has the best of both worlds. The Mike Quon Design Office — always humming with activity — is only minutes away from his home. He has reclaimed his personal space, but still maintains a small home studio. Complete with fax machine, drawing table and other tools of the trade, but isolated from the hustle and bustle of the office, the loft has become a decidedly easier place to work these days.

phoned and went over the next day with his portfolio. "After my presentation I was asked to return the following day to pick up a project," he remembers. "I couldn't believe my ears. It was my first time out in the cold-calling business!" Mike Quon's design business was off and running and has moved at a sprint ever since.

Quon was prompted by this suc-

His combination of sharp sales skills, promotional savvy, and obvious talent and ability soon kicked his new business into high gear. But as his business grew, Quon sometimes found up to 10 free-lancers (six of them full-time) working in his home. "It was too crazy," he recalls. "The loft was no longer a place where I could *live*. Every inch of space was used for

Whether you are wishing to move in, up or out, Quon — with the hindsight and wisdom of someone who's been there — advises considering these questions first:

"Do you want the pressure of a debt load?" (Quon invested savings plus small personal and business loans into furnishings and renovation.) "Does your situation warrant a move and can your business sustain such a move? Are you being realistic about the economy and the state of future business? What are the indicators of your continued success? Are there outside forces or changes that may side-track your master plan?"

He also recommends, "Don't overspend. Don't overbuild. Be cautious as you expand — take small steps. Avoid runaway growth. Keep your overhead low. Think flexibility — plan ahead for expansion. It's amazing how much storage and work space is needed for this type of business.

"Have alternatives, just in case. Seek advice, get good counsel and listen. Network. Nobody knows how to inherently build a new office space. It's trial and error. Remember . . . it's important to dream, and stay flexible for growth."

Quon's promotion pieces have changed over the years as his studio has grown and acquired new clients, but he's kept his distinctive logo (upper left corner). The logo he created while still in college is used on his letterhead, T-shirts, mugs, a neon sign, and as an integral part of many promotions.

This early Quon postcard was part of his most successful self-promotional campaign — in his travels around the world, he photographed people with his logo, producing truly memorable results. The juxtaposition of Australian aborigines and Egyptian temple worshippers with Quon's logo made people laugh — and got Quon noticed. He cautions fellow designers from sending postcards too often, though — "you don't want to appear to be away all the time."

CHAPTER 4

DEVELOPING YOUR FINANCIAL PLANS

You need to have a financial plan. It's dangerous to start out underfinanced, yet you don't want to spend too much money at first.

In this chapter we'll assess how much money you will need, how much you can realistically plan to earn and where and how to get the needed capital. You'll also find out how to create a working budget to maintain a cash flow that will keep your business in the black.

Step 1: Figure Out How Much Money You'll Need

Get a handle on just what it will cost you to be in business by figuring out first what your start-up expenses will be. This would include all one-time expenses involved in beginning a business. Factor in fixtures, equipment and installation; office supplies, decorating and remodeling; rent, phone and utilities deposits; legal and professional fees; licenses and permits; advertising and promotion; and operating cash.

The bottom half of the start-up worksheet at the right can be adapted to fit your needs and give you an accurate picture of what it will cost to get your firm off the ground.

Fixed and Variable Expenses

After calculating start-up costs, you'll need to figure out what your expenses will be on a monthly basis

and enter them on the top half of the start-up worksheet. You can break this down into monthly, fixed expenses: rent, utilities, loan payments, parking, your salary (if any), etc. Add to these, your variable operating expenses or what you think it costs on a per month basis for items such as supplies, postage, entertainment and transportation. If you have purchases that will need to be made only once or twice a year (for example, you estimate a roll of acetate will last you about 12 months), take the cost of the roll and divide it by 12 to come up with the monthly cost for this item. Do this with the rest of your equipment and supply costs, and you should have a pretty good idea of what your monthly expenses will be.

Don't include items such as typesetting, photography, printing or illustration in your monthly tally. These job expenses should be billed to the client for each job they are purchased for. An exception would be service expenses incurred for your own promotional pieces. Here the typesetting, photography, printing or illustration charges *are* operating expenses and should be factored into the equation.

Step 2: Estimate How Much You Think You'll Earn

You have a number of potential clients with a certain amount of busi-

ness to give you. Think about their needs, and how you can fulfill them in order to get a realistic picture of how much and what kind of work you could be doing for them.

Finding Your Business Potential

Based on the soul searching you did earlier in this book, you should now have some idea of what skills

START-UP COSTS		
Monthly	**Estimate**	**Actual**
Rent or mortgage		
Legal		
Adv. and Promotion		
Supplies and Materials		
Acct./Bookkeeping		
Other professional fees		
Insurance		
Owner's draw		
Shipping and delivery		
Telephone/Fax		
Utilities		
Loan and interest		
Maintenance/cleaning		
Auto/travel		
Other		
Subtotal		
One-time only	**Estimate**	**Actual**
Operating cash		
Licenses and permits		
Deposit for Utilities		
Decorating/Remodeling		
Fixtures and equipment		
Installation of Equip.		
Rent Deposit		
Legal Consult.		
Accountant Consult.		
Initial Adv./Promo.		
Miscellaneous		
Subtotal		
Total cash needed		

This worksheet will help you figure out such initial expenses as deposits for utilities or printing letterhead, and ongoing expenses such as supplies and materials or telephone bills.

Keep your overhead low in the beginning years. Be ready to do most of the work yourself. You're going to have to wear all the hats, so discipline is incredibly important.

Rex Peteet, Sibley/Peteet Design

you should be marketing, and where they can best be applied. Whether you'll be pitching brochures or four-color ads, you'll need to have a practical estimate of how much business you can expect, and where it will come from.

Start by thinking how you can build on existing business. Let's assume that one of your prospective clients is starting a business and that you're going to be developing a logo for him. Certainly there's the potential for developing other business and promotional materials as well. Are there other clients out there for whom you could be doing similar work? Do you stand a good chance of building this business through referrals? Is there a good possibility you could be doing a substantial amount of logo or identity work? If this is the case, make a list. Project how many logo jobs you think will come to you in a given year. At a cost of $800 each (if this is what you think your average charge will be), what does this come to annually? Figure from there how much of this business will spin off into collateral work for

each of your logo clients and attach a monetary value to all of it.

Do the same for any other type of work you think you will be doing. Figure out how much business in this area you may realistically get, as well as what you are capable of doing in a year. Think in terms of projects on an annual basis, and after you have made a list and totaled it, divide this figure by 12 to get an idea of what your monthly gross profit will be.

Step 3: Can You Make Ends Meet?

You will need to compare costs and income to see if your business plan is viable. A lowball or highball scheme built around inaccuracies won't get you very far in practice, so make sure your projections reflect real world facts and figures.

Bone up! Research the numbers by talking to both buyers and sellers of graphic design. Compare notes with your professional friends; brainstorm with family. Hit the library and bookstore to study pertinent texts.

Create a Hypothetical Budget

A budget is *important*. It's absolutely vital that you have a handle on expenses and income—and it's best to have it on paper. Otherwise, you'll have no idea how you're doing financially (and why) or where your money is going.

Check out the budget template on page 51. Doing just the "estimate" column would give you what's called a cash flow statement or budget projection. You could do a monthly, quarterly or yearly projection using our format. On the yearly projection, you could also tack on a preopening column, if you desire. Use the "actual" column to gauge how good your estimates are and fine tune future projections.

Calculate Your Break-Even Point

Here's a formula you can use to calculate your break-even point. Let's assume that your expenses add up to $2,000 per month. You know that every week you have to bill $500 worth of design fees to break even (or $2,000 every month). The break-even point is the amount you have to bring in for your business to survive. It's pretty simple math. If you want to end up with a $12,000 profit at the end of the year, figure on billing $3,000 every month or $750 every week.

You can take this formula a step further and figure out your billable rate as well. If you can manage 25 billable hours out of every week

This budget worksheet will help you see how much money you must make to cover your expenses—or how little you can afford to spend. First, estimate how much actual cash you will have on hand each month. When in doubt, go low. Then divide up your cash to cover projected expenses. If you can't make ends meet on paper, you won't in real life either. Keep refiguring your expenses until you get a workable result. Once you're up and running, track your *actual* expenses and see how your budget is working. If you're making more money than you expected, congratulations! Gradually increase your expenses, but leave yourself some money at month's end for your nest egg. If you're making less than expected or expenses are higher, bite the bullet and decrease your expenses quickly.

1991 Budget	Month:	Estimate	Actual	Estimate	Actual
INCOME:	Cash on hand, first of month				
	Receipts				
	Loans				
	Savings				
	A. Total Cash Available				
EXPENSES:	Rent/Mortgage				
	Health/Life/Business Insurance				
	Supplies and Materials				
	Shipping				
	Utilities				
	Telephone/Fax				
	Repairs/Maintenance				
	Legal				
	Travel/Transportation				
	Meals and Entertainment				
	Adv. and Promotion				
	Equipment				
	Cleaning				
	Dues and Publications				
	Accounting/Bookkeeping				
	Other				
	Subtotal				
	Loan Payment With Interest				
	Owner's Draw				
	Capital Purchases (depreciated items)				
	B. Total Cash Paid Out				
	Subtract Total B from Total A (+ or −)				

(it's reasonable to assume that you can squeeze five billable hours of work out of every day) you will need to bill your time at $30 per hour in order to cover expenses and achieve your goal of a $12,000 profit at the end of the year.

Of course, all of this figuring is done on an average basis. It's impractical to assume that you will bill $750 on a regular basis. More than likely, you won't bill a cent during some weeks, and then bill a number of projects within a given week to make up for the previous week's slack. This is why it makes

We met with an accountant and created a plan. A financial plan forces you to be realistic. It makes you put down on paper what you think your overhead is really going to be, how much it's going to take to meet that overhead and make enough money to live on. A plan helps you focus and organize. It would have been kind of frightening to have never gone through that process or do it the day we opened our doors.

Don Sibley, Sibley/Peteet Design

more sense to figure out what your income will be on an annual basis and then divide this figure by 12 to balance this against your monthly expenses.

Step 4: Getting the Money You Need

When most people consider possible cash sources they think first of borrowing from the bank. Yes, a bank loan is a possibility, but the chances are, at best, slim. To explain why, we'll detail the process of getting a bank loan. We'll explore what's involved in proving the viability of your business and establishing your credit and credibility — in short, convincing the bank to loan you money. We'll look at some other possibilities for obtaining capital, too.

Banks

Let's be frank, up front, right now. When you ask for a loan, the first question a bank may ask you is, "Why did you quit your full-time job?" Sit down — here are some other facts of life when it comes to banks and loan acquisition.

Banks look upon a freelancer as a rather unstable commodity and are well aware that new businesses frequently fail. Lenders are hesitant, especially in today's economy, to loan any money to a service business because, frankly, there's nothing they can touch should the business go belly-up. You won't be able to use your fledgling design studio as collateral for that same reason.

If it's a nonsecured loan, a bank will be unwilling to "give" you money unless you can bring other assets to the table — a car, your house (a second home mortgage), a working spouse (as cosigner), the birthright to your next-born child (only kidding, I think).

If you can get a bank loan, you will have to personally guarantee it (even your vaunted corporation status may not exclude you). You may also face sky-high interest rates or unfavorable terms.

What all this means is that your chances of obtaining a loan as a freelancer or new small business owner drop automatically. But don't totally eliminate the possibility of obtaining a bank loan at some point in the future, after your business is established (you'll find more information on this and how to qualify in chapter six).

Somewhere down the road, your great reputation will be well earned through quality work. You will have cultivated a cozy rapport with your banker and built a solid credit history with a positive net worth. You'll hold substantial security, and, of course, the studio will be turning business away. You may then have a good chance at getting that loan. But even then, it's no sure thing (and you'll probably still have to personally guarantee the debt).

What to Expect When You Apply
There are certain criteria a lender will use to determine if you're a good risk. Let's say you have one golden minute to state your case. What would a lender want to know in sixty seconds? She'll ask five basic (but oh, so big) questions:

- What is the service or product you're trying to sell?
- What is your experience and track record?
- Who are you and what is your credit history?
- What is your ability to repay the loan?
- What is your security or collateral for the loan?

The first two questions are the icebreakers, but questions three, four and five are the nutcrackers — the ones the loan officer really cares about. These are the fabled "three C's," representing character, capacity and collateral.

If you have a checkered past with a dubious credit history, that's bad character. If you don't look like you have a good way to repay the debt, that's poor capacity. If you can't bring enough security to cover it, that's inadequate collateral. You're not going to get the loan if you rate poorly in all categories — it's that simple.

Credit Ratings
You might want to keep tabs on your credit rating by sending for a credit report from agencies such as

TRW, Trans Union and Credit Bureau. You can find these services in the Yellow Pages. As of this writing, this will cost about $20.

TRW has announced that as of April, 1992, consumers can receive one free copy of their report each year. Write to TRW's National Consumer Relations Center, 12606 Greenville Ave., P.O. Box 749029, Dallas, TX 75374-9029 or call (214) 235-1200 (ext. 251).

Even if you have a perfect credit record, sometimes wrong information can end up in your credit file, so get a credit report before applying for a loan to ensure that you won't be turned down. Refusals become part of your credit history and several refusals will look bad in your credit report. If you are ever turned down for a loan, make sure you get the name of the credit bureau your lender used. The lender is required by law to make this information available to you, and the credit bureau, likewise, is legally obligated to tell you over the phone, free-of-charge, what is in your credit report.

Beyond the Bank: Other Loan Options

We can conservatively estimate that it's going to take six to 12 months (or more) of working capital for a start-up business to survive. This is without spending a dollar generated by that business (and don't forget—you'll need living expenses, too). What are some sources of additional funds? A bank may be the first place to start because you want to develop a relationship with a banker as you start growing your studio, but remember: If you're fresh off the bus with no client base, experience, savings or equity, your chances are pretty slim. Here are some alternatives:

• **Personal reserves:** Tap into your own savings for start-up money. The way to build a nest egg is to sock away as much money as you can while you're still employed.

• **Loans from family and friends:** The interest rates and terms are usually great and you're intimately acquainted with your "banker." Should there be problems, you know the lender is looking out for your best interests. However, this is still a business loan, to be repaid in a timely manner. Writing up a formal document might be a good idea.

• **Credit unions:** These people-oriented, nonprofit co-ops generally stay away from commercial investments and business loans. But, if you're a member and meet the criteria, a credit union would give you an unsecured (often called a personal or "signature") loan. Most credit unions will look at your employment record, check your credit rating and membership status (you should be a member for at least one year) and will calculate your debt-to-income ratio.

• **Borrow against your life insurance policy:** If you have enough equity, this is a relatively easy way to get some cash. Like any loan, there is interest involved, but the rate is usually very reasonable.

At our bank presentations we presented our two-year, pro forma (based on the work we felt we could realistically get through contacts), promised receivables as collateral, and personally guaranteed the loan. We even took our portfolio along. However, we found that they weren't really concerned about the creative end. Basically, what they were interested in was our ability to make good on the loan—they wanted to know what our personal and financial situations were.

Don Sibley, Sibley/Peteet Design

And understand that if the loan is not repaid before your untimely demise, the debt would be deducted from your benefits.

• **Borrow against your savings:** Use your savings as the collateral for a loan (thus creating a secured loan). What you are doing is borrowing your own money (and know that you'll be paying interest on the use of money you already have).

In this situation, your account balance and your loan balance must be the same. As you repay the loan, the principal goes down, allowing you to then dip back into your savings. The lender won't let you fall below the loan balance. (They'll put a hold on your savings before that happens.) If for some reason you can't make the payments, your savings will be used to pay off the loan.

• **Get a partner and pool resources:** Some designers swear by their partners; some swear at them. For a more detailed discussion of partnerships, see pages 19-20.

• **Small Business Administration:** If you qualify, this might be just the ticket.

• **Commercial finance or credit companies:** Your junk mail is already seeded with mailers from such places. Yes, you'll find attractive, flexible plans, but you'll also find short-term secured loans with higher interest rates. And expect the lenders to be more interested in that collateral (as in "easily liqui-

The Small Business Administration

Small Business Administration loans are usually done through a bank, but they don't look at loans much under $100,000 (they'll just refer you right back to your financial institution). The SBA describes a small business as "one that is independently owned and operated, and not dominant in its field." Eligibility for a loan is based on size, need and, in a sense, desperation — you must prove that you can't get financing anywhere else. There is also a minority loan program, special SBA loans for Vietnam veterans and women, and a program for handicapped individuals.

The SBA primarily grants what's called a guaranty loan. Let's think positive: a lender thinks you're OK and your application is forwarded to the SBA, which approves it. They guarantee up to 90 percent of a five to seven year loan at an interest rate negotiated between lender and borrower, and within SBA guidelines. Bingo! The lender gives you the cash.

How does one apply? Write for the official SBA guidelines; but in the meantime, here's how it basically works:

Step 1. The SBA will ask,

"What are you buying? What's it going to cost?"

Step 2. You present to the bank:

• Current balance sheets;
• Past and present profit and loss statements;
• Personal, owners' and major stockholders' financial statements;
• Three years of financial projections;
• Work history (and expertise); and
• Last but not least, your collateral.

Step 3. The lender then decides to submit the paperwork to the SBA. While you may not meet the bank's criteria on your own, you just might if you're backed by the SBA's guarantee.

Step 4. The SBA approves or turns you down.

Contact the SBA for a variety of publications and assistance:

Office of Public Communication, U.S. Small Business Administration, Mail Code: 2550, 1441 L Street NW, Washington, D.C. 20416. Find the SBA office near you by calling their national toll free number: (800) 857-5722.

dated") than the health of your business. If you want or need the money badly enough, go ahead, but go in with your eyes open.

• **Credit cards:** Convenient, but inadvisable because of high interest rates (16 to 25 percent). Think of credit cards just for short-term financing. You can build a credit history with credit cards, but be aware that a bad rating means trouble when establishing credit with vendors or looking for a loan.

Although a loan may be out of reach initially, look ahead. Form a relationship with your bank as you shape your business. While a bank loan might be hard to get at first, it may be a different story once you've established credit, a good reputation and a solid business.

The road to landing a loan is rough, even for established designers who've been around the block a few times. With a start-up, it just might be an impossible dream.

they've checked your references—and you check out—they will extend credit (another great reason to pay your bills on time).

Step 5: Seek an Accountant's Advice

If you're just starting out, you should hire (or at the very least, consult) an accountant.

A good accountant can be the linchpin of your business. He or she can review your situation and tell you if you need a lawyer, and then make recommendations and referrals. An accountant can apprise you of government regulations, set up your bookkeeping system, and be your financial advisor and tax consultant/preparer.

Find a person you can rely on year-round—don't be tempted to hire a moonlighter around tax time. You'll need to find someone who is well qualified and whom you can trust, because ultimately you will be responsible for this individual's mistakes. You may think you will save some money by going to "Taxes 'R Us" for your tax return. However, it could cost you much more in IRS penalties when you find out what Ronald Maccountant didn't understand about tax law. As a designer with a new business, I'd go to a public accountant, an enrolled agent, or a CPA specializing in accounting and tax preparation for small businesses.

What's the SCORE?

Sponsored by the SBA, SCORE stands for the Service Corps of Retired Executives. It's a volunteer organization of men and women who counsel small businesses at start-up and offer business education programs. It can be a great clearinghouse for a wealth of information from local professionals. As these folks have been there, they know and can help a small business through the rough spots too. And guess what—their services are free!

To locate and contact your local SCORE office, simply check the phone or call the SBA at their national toll free number: (800) 857-5722.

Don't Give Up

If you're still employed and want to start your own business, you might apply for a loan while you still have a job and start your business as a moonlighter. A bank may look at your day job as the capacity to repay a loan. Freelance on the side and grow your business as you grow your bank account. Eventually use this reliability, experience, track record and equity to show a bank you're a good risk.

Establishing Credit With Vendors and Suppliers

You will want to establish credit with suppliers such as printers, typesetters and supply houses. The best way to do this is simple, short and sweet: pay up and on time.

If you're trying to get credit, many vendors will ask you to fill out a credit form. This form asks where you do your banking and for references (two or three vendors you've used in the past). Once

Your accountant is probably the centerpiece of it all. An accountant can refer you to most of the other professionals. A designer can do his own bookkeeping, but you don't want to deal with tax situations on your own. For that reason alone, an accountant is a mainstay of your operation.

Tom Nicholson, Tom Nicholson Associates, Inc.

Why Not Do It Yourself?

So you bought a green eyeshade and you're going to do your own tax return. Here are four well chosen words: I'd advise against it. I can even make it simpler: *Don't!* Personal tax preparation is elaborate enough. Due to your start-up situation, you could make some mistakes; there may be some advantages or requirements, penalties or benefits of which you might not be aware. Besides, you're a designer, not an accountant. Maybe you can handle the job, but you really don't have the expertise to do it right. And finally, how much creative work will you accomplish away from the board, and what's your time worth?

How to Choose an Accountant

You'll want to find an accountant with small business experience and possibly someone who's familiar with graphic design firms. It's best to get referrals from others in your situation who have a comparable income to your own.

There are four basic levels of experience that you can use in gauging the expertise of anyone you're interested in hiring:

• **Accountant:** Usually has a four-year degree in accounting, but doesn't necessarily have to have any training (not to mention a degree, license or track record). Anyone can call himself an accountant—just like anyone can call herself a designer.

• **Enrolled Agent:** Certified by the IRS itself (but does not work for the government). Upon meeting official requirements and passing an exam, enrolled agents are the only other individuals (along with lawyers and CPAs) authorized to represent clients before the Internal Revenue Service.

• **Public Accountant:** Usually has a two- or four-year degree in accounting and is licensed by the state. He or she has probably passed a practical exam in the areas of accounting and tax, but each

state will have different rules and regulations regarding who can call himself a public accountant.

• **Certified Public Accountant:** The highest degree of professional accreditation. A CPA has a four- or five-year degree in accounting and at least one year of public accounting experience. Most important, all CPAs must pass a rigorous exam.

Once you've found at least three candidates, interview them and evaluate each by considering:

• **Rapport:** Could you work with this individual? Do you like her? Do you like her style? Do you trust her?

• **Communication:** Can you understand him? Is his advice clear? Does he understand you? Will he fully comprehend both your personal and business needs?

• **Expertise:** Check this individual's credentials. But also prepare questions and present data relevant to your business scenario. Do his or her recommendations make sense for your situation?

• **Fee:** Finally, find out what this individual's fee will be for general advice, preparing quarterly reviews of your tax situation, and preparing a tax return. You will also want to find out if this individual will work with your bank, lawyer and your financial planner.

Financial Planning Comes First

Like many of her classmates at the University of Cincinnati, Lori Siebert dreamed of opening her own design business. "It was my goal throughout school," she comments. At that point, the dedicated, energetic, but practical Siebert theorized that her objective would not be realized for some time.

Siebert worked at a local studio for a couple of years, and then went on to a job as art director for a national trade magazine. Working on a magazine staff instead of at a design studio had its advantages: "I was able to freelance on the side because there was no conflict of interest," says Siebert. Her moonlighting helped build the client base that would be the mainstay of her fledgling business.

Freelancing and then starting her own business was a natural progression for a cutting-edge designer working in the conservative Cincinnati area. "Not many places were doing the type of work I wanted to do," recalls Siebert, "and there just weren't many people doing what I was doing." The fact that she was doing a kind of design work unique for her community gave her a distinct advantage over more conventional designers in the area: She had an open market and many opportunities for making her design style highly visible in pro bono projects for the arts.

Through her freelancing and her pro bono work, Siebert created a niche for herself in Cincinnati; her brand of design quickly caught on. It soon became apparent that her freelance business was growing to the point where it was becoming almost a full-time business. The high visibility she acquired after receiving a number of awards from her local art directors club—and the ensuing increase in freelance business that came from this recognition—prompted Siebert to start her own design firm in 1987, just three short years after graduating. "My father and husband said at the time, 'Why don't we look at whether or not there's a viable business here?'" says Siebert.

Siebert's father, an accountant, first drew up a profit and loss projection, in which her freelance sales and her cost of doing business were anticipated for the coming year. Many of Siebert's projections for job-related expenses were ascertained from the expenses incurred on previous work, as well as anticipated new expenses. Nonproject-related costs included her start-up expenses and customary business expenses (rent, phone bill, travel, entertainment and parking expenses).

Siebert based her profit projections on her past and current freelance sales. She assumed this income would modestly increase over the next 12 months as she made the transition from billing on a part-time to full-time basis. Based

on this estimation, she received a $5,000 loan from her father to cover the initial cost of renting studio space and start-up materials and supplies.

In addition to figuring in what she needed to pay for ongoing supplies, services and rent, Siebert also drew a modest salary for herself. Although she never officially calculated a break-even point for her business, Siebert had originally planned to pay back her father's loan gradually (over the course of a year's time, with whatever money was left over at the end of each month). But business was better than she anticipated, and she was able to pay back the loan in just six short months.

In fact, business was coming in so quickly, Siebert had to bring in another freelance designer after just two months of being on her own. Within a short time, this designer was putting in 40 hours a week. To save money, Siebert had no choice but to make her a full-time salaried employee just five months after starting her studio.

Although Siebert blew her profit projections out of the water, she does recall having a problem with cash flow, a concern that still warrants vigilance and perseverance when it comes to collections. The studio tries to maintain a 30 to 45 day payment policy and now requires one-third of a project's fee up front before starting business with new clients. For Siebert, as with many start-up businesses, a few slow-paying accounts can have a major impact on a budget. Lack of available funds can quickly bring things to a halt even when clients are clamoring for your services. Siebert recently brought her husband Steve into the firm to help manage finances on a full-time basis. Steve Siebert and his father-in-law make a point of coming up with a cash flow projection every year and base their growth strategies on this projection. They review their annual projection every three months to be sure the current situation is in line with their original projections, and revise their plan and future projections, if necessary.

Because of this planning (along with her considerable talent) Siebert's growth has been remarkable, netting profits that have doubled every year for her first four years of doing business. She currently employs a staff of seven and grosses over a half million annually in sales.

As far as the future is concerned, Siebert remarks, "I want to grow in sales, not in size. I'd like to weed out my nonprofitable clients but not my nonprofit clientele." Siebert plans to continue doing pro bono work for the creative freedom it offers. "I want to delete some of the rather mundane work and aggressively market in more targeted areas," she adds. "I want to continue to find ongoing client relationships."

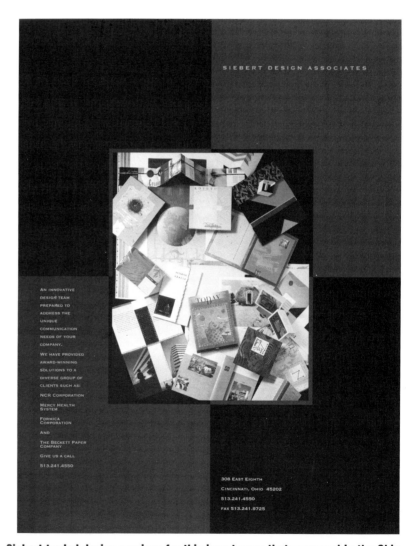

Siebert traded design services for this insert page that appeared in the Ohio Sourcebook. The page shows the breadth of work done by Siebert Design Associates. The studio not only appeared in the book but also received extra copies to use for future self-promotion. This trade was an economical way of marketing the studio's services.

Bennett Peji

Walking the High Wire

Bennett Peji says, "Being in business for yourself is sometimes like walking the high wire without a net. You have to be very good to make it or. . . . " He deliberately leaves the sentence "hanging" so the listener will complete this striking and appropriate metaphor.

Peji walks that wire every day out

of his offices at Bennett Peji Design, in La Jolla, California. Indeed, you might say that when he set up shop, he did his act blindfolded, for Peji gave it a shot right after graduating from San Diego State University in 1987. Today, his company is an internationally recognized firm. Peji not only makes it across the perilous chasm safely; he does it with style, grace and great skill.

"I figured that starting a business straight out of school was a natural time to make the move since I had minimal responsibilities, except to myself. If I failed, no

one would suffer but me," Peji recalls. "I worked out of my home to keep overhead low." Peji moved to his own place of business in 1988. He invested his own personal savings of $5,000 in a computer and other basic equipment.

Peji was able to acquire a couple of clients immediately after he graduated through networking. "I attended every design function I could and networked. At presentations, I 'looked the part' — I 'dressed for success' and bought a briefcase for my material. I priced appropriately and asked the right fees . . . if I walked in somewhere with my nice suit and fancy briefcase, and then quoted $200 for a logo, I'd have been laughed out of the place."

But Peji says that the reason he was able to make it was because he took small steps. "I never overextended myself — never took a bigger step than I had saved or earned for." He also was careful to ensure that he had adequate cash flow and clients that he knew were serious about paying for the work he was contracted to do. He asked for payment up front and billed incrementally while a job was in progress. "I collected 50 percent up front. People don't take you seriously if you don't expect payment for your work," he points out. Peji says that he also refused to work on spec for the same reason.

"Working on spec is essentially giving away your design," he cautions. "Your ideas are your most valuable asset. I try to educate potential clients that a designer only does this when he or she is less experienced, less capable, and simply has the time to do free work."

Peji concentrates on preparing a solid proposal that convinces a client he or she is making a sound investment and getting a good value (based on his previous work, portfolio and case histories). "This is a tall order," he admits. "Basically you have to convince someone to trust you, to pay money up front for work not yet done."

Peji stresses the importance of pricing work appropriately to achieve the kind of cash flow that will maintain a viable business. "It's easy to freelance for a couple of years with minimal overhead. But when it becomes a career your prices have to go up. That's the pivotal point — does the work justify the increased rates? When you demand what the cream of the crop charge, are you still going to get work?"

Peji gets the work. Although he has been increasing his rates annually, business has just about doubled every year. "However, my accountant still says I'm not charging enough," Peji smiles. This steady growth has transformed a novice into a competent manager. An or-

Bennett Peji's business forms cover all the necessary details to help the business side of his studio run smoothly. The agreement form spells out what will be done, what it will cost, and when payment is expected. The invoice picks up where the agreement leaves off. Both forms are not only functional but attractive.

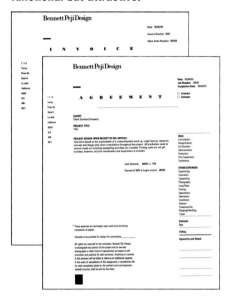

ganized and logical individual by nature, Peji has found these traits essential to running a successful and *efficient* business. "Of course," he adds, "getting sound advice from my accountant and friends, as well as other established designers, saved me from having to learn many things the hard way."

Another key factor of Peji's continued good fortune is his ability to communicate with clients, to articulate ideas in a concrete, factual manner. Peji is thus able to tailor presentations from a marketing standpoint — he can offer design solutions in terms of how these an-

swers will benefit the client's bottom line. "I have the ability to put myself in my clients' shoes, to see from their standpoint what *they* are looking for," he says.

He also approaches each project as an opportunity to begin a long-term client/designer relationship, not as a one-time job. "A designer must set up a situation, through his work, by her case histories, that says 'I'm the expert — let me do my job.' However, it's crucial to get the client involved, to establish their ownership. Never go to the extreme — 'Here, take it or leave it.' You may sell them on a single project, but if clients don't feel their ownership in the process, they won't want to continue with you.

"This concern about benefits for my clients over the long haul has resulted in referrals from every client I've worked with," Peji says. "My business grows as their business grows."

Business has indeed grown. "I actually was profitable after my first year," Peji recalls, "and I realized that my business was viable when I saw that clients were staying with me — not only continuing with the work but giving me referrals as well.

"Going into business fresh out of school, not really having any credentials or credibility, the only validation I got from a design standpoint was from competitions. Regardless of how short or long you've been around, there are out-

lets to evaluate your design against the best in the country (or the world). Anybody, at any time, can see how bona fide their stuff is — if it stands up to the work of their peers — through this gauge."

Peji is the recipient of numerous awards, including those from *Graphis*, The Art Directors Club of Los Angeles, and the Type Directors Club (New York), *Print*, *HOW* and *Art Direction* magazines; his quality work has been recognized by both peers and pundits. He makes walking that high wire look easy.

Peji's ability to communicate with clients such as Culinary Production, the catering and special events company whose logo is shown here, is one key to his success. Another is his ability to run an effective, efficient business.

Kim Youngblood

Planning for Success

"The whole reason for my being in communications, as opposed to fine arts, was because I liked the idea of being paid for what I did," says Kim Youngblood of Youngblood, Sweat and Tears. "The economics fascinated me."

Indeed. "When I was in the fourth grade, I designed a hall bulletin board at school, then charged my classmates to see it," the Atlanta designer laughs. "I would do portraits of the neighborhood kids and sell them for a quarter," she reminisces. "I understood at a very early age that there's value in the creative process."

According to Youngblood, this is a lesson artistic adults must also heed. "Many graphic designers set themselves up for a fall by not effecting a perceived value for their work," she points out. "Too many designers are also guilty of not providing that left brain function and come across as being flaky and irresponsible. This might be OK for the fine art world where there are no parameters, but designers today are called upon to be strategic partners."

"Designers are now being made accountable — they must understand who the target audience is and what the client's objectives are. These days, we must design more for an end result that's relevant — not just to design something that's decorative and wins awards."

Given the success of her eight-year-old firm, it's easy to see how the junior art entrepreneur grew up to be a most astute and savvy businessperson. At the helm of a seven-person staff, Youngblood saw her company quadruple in growth since 1985. However, she eventually realized that she wanted to divest herself of administrative responsibilities. Youngblood longed to concentrate on the creative process. "I needed to get out of billing conferences and into strategic meetings," she recalls. "I wanted to get back on the board and do what I do best.

"I can do one or the other, but my heart is in the creative — that's where my gift is, where my passion lies. However, I'm not throwing all that business-oriented stuff away. A great account executive must understand the creative end of things. Likewise, a creative person needs to know the business side," Youngblood says, "but they usually don't broadcast this. As a responsible leader and a communications professional, I have to know the business," and she laughs, "but I try to keep it a secret!"

In 1991, Youngblood sold her company to the Atlanta-based advertising firm of Fitzgerald & Co. "Originally, my goal was to bring in a managing partner," she says. "Someone to build our business, to do the administrative end. We were working with more sophisticated and demanding clients, so more challenging marketing thinking was needed.

"Larger clients (like Amoco, Turner Broadcasting, the Marriott Corporation) demanded more time, more strategic partnering. Their demands grew to require the addition of a veteran, high-level strategic thinker. What evolved was an actual merger with a larger ad agency, and then we brought on an executive vice president/general manager, Sal Kibler, a year later." Since Youngblood sold her company to Fitzgerald & Co., she is on salary with a percentage of the profits. The YST staff has remained (and grown), and the firm moved to big, new "Class A" offices (on the same floor as Fitzgerald), but maintains its own entrance and separate space.

"This is another chapter in the life of Youngblood, Sweat and Tears," says Youngblood. "It's just a natural part of our growth curve. I have aligned myself with a marketing-oriented ad agency, because we have always been a marketing-oriented design firm. We're providing the next level of service and keeping up with the times—integrated marketing. Integrated marketing is the area where graphic design meets advertising meets public relations meets media planning."

This ad maker knows the magic and innovation of the creative process and says, "You can't have a business without the fun, the desire, the soul. But you can't have this spirit unless it's supported financially. You have to have the heart *and* the head. The most important thing about running a successful creative business is that balance."

Kim Youngblood has always made pro bono work a part of Youngblood, Sweat and Tears's business. She is active in many Atlanta civic, charitable and professional organizations. Her pro bono work gives her the chance to benefit her community and the opportunity to demonstrate her studio's creative talents before a wide audience.

CHAPTER 5

PRICING YOUR WORK AND GETTING PAID

Society calls creative professionals **ARTISTS** (in big, bold, capital letters). Artists do what they do for a variety of reasons: for personal satisfaction, for public recognition or the respect of their peers, for the sheer fun of it, for posterity, or—dare we say it—simply for the bucks. Now I believe most artists would work without getting paid—for love, as it were—but as **BUSINESSPEOPLE** (also in big, bold capitals) this would be *ruin*.

Like it or not, graphic designers must be businesspeople. So this chapter deals with pricing your work. We'll discuss how to be adequately compensated for your time, making a proposal, writing contracts and letters of agreement, and collecting your money.

Step 1: Pricing Your Work

What do you charge when you're just starting out? Your fee will most probably come down to answering these three questions:

- How much should you charge?
- How much could you charge?
- How much do you want to charge?

Think of these questions as the basic rules of thumb. Coming up with a pricing strategy that answers all of these points will help you know how to charge a fair price for your work. For a pricing strategy to succeed, both buyer and seller

Your clients want a good designer. They want somebody who can really do what they need and who they can work with. If they have one designer who's willing to do it for $32,000 and another designer who's willing to do it for $40,000, most clients, I believe, are smart enough to not necessarily go with the lower price.

Tibor Kalman, M & Co.

should demand these three things:

- A definite price,
- A fair price,
- A competitive price.

How do you arrive at a value for your time that meets all of these criteria? You could charge by the project, knowing how a similar job has been priced out in the past (or by knowing what the competition is charging). Or you can arrive at an hourly fee based on your project expenses and the expenses you incur in the course of doing business.

Figure Out What to Charge for Your Time

You'll remember that in chapter four we discussed how to figure out what your break-even point will be. Let's review, in more detail, how to arrive at an hourly rate based on your start-up and variable expenses. Look again at the budget template on page 51 and refer to it when calculating what your ex-

penses will be.

Let's assume the following as an example of monthly expenses:

Mortgage/Rent	$ 300
Repairs/Maintenance	30
Licenses/Permits/Taxes	400
Utilities	150
Materials/Supplies	50
Shipping/Postage	50
Telephone/Fax	125
Travel/Transportation	50
Meals/Entertainment	75
Advertising/Promotion	30
Equipment	125
Accounting/Legal Fees	60
Salary	2,500
Total Monthly	
Operating Costs	**$3,945**
Start-up Costs	**$3,000**

Take your monthly total from above and plug it into the following formula:

- Multiply your monthly operating costs by 12.
  $3,945 \times 12 = $47,340
- Add start-up costs.

$47,340 + $3,000 = $50,340

- Divide this figure by 52 to get the weekly cost of doing business.

  $50,340 \div 52 = $968.08

- Divide your weekly total by 5 to get your daily total.

  $968.08 \div 5 = $193.62

- Divide daily total by 5 (the average number of billable hours most people can get out of a working day) to get your hourly rate.

  $193.62 \div 5 = $38.72

This represents the absolute minimum you must charge as your hourly rate in order to break even. Remember, this is your break-even point — it doesn't take into account time off for vacation or sick leave nor does it figure in any kind of a profit margin.

However, let's assume that you wanted to realize a $12,000 profit at the end of the year. You can break this annual figure down with the formula given above and then add it to your hourly rate as follows:

- Divide $12,000 by 52 to come up with a weekly figure.

  $12,000 \div 52 = $230.77

- Divide $230.77 by 5 to come up with a daily figure.

  $230.77 \div 5 = $46.15

- Divide $46.15 by 5 to come up with hourly rate.

  $46.15 \div 5 = $9.23

- Add $9.23 to your hourly break-even rate of $38.72 in order to come up with an average hourly billing fee that will give you a comfortable profit margin.

  $38.72 + $9.23 = $47.95

In order to cover the expenses of doing business and realize a $12,000 profit at the end of the year, you will need to charge, on the average, $47.95 per hour for your time and bill an average of five hours per day.

Charging by the Project

You may also want to determine, on a per project basis, what fee you think you will need to be fairly compensated for the job. Let's assume your client is willing to spend $1,500 for a four-page, 11-by-17-inch four-color brochure. First estimate and deduct production costs ($450 for printing, $300 for color separations, $150 for typesetting and stats, which means a total of $900). After the $900 for production costs has been deducted, you're left with $600 as compensation for labor, or your time on the job. If you divide this by your

---

Working on Spec

XYZ company has a plum assignment. The art director gives you a buzz to say that they're also considering three other designers around town. Your studio is definitely in the running, but XYZ is asking all concerned to do a spec layout for evaluation.

You may agree to do this little freebie in the obvious hopes that you'll land the account, but most designers will tell you that this is a mistake. I agree. You're working for nothing, with no guarantee that you'll get paid. If the client likes your concept, maybe — just maybe — you'll get the job (and with competition, the odds only get worse). Speculative work is hardly unethical — it just isn't cost-effective or time-efficient for a busy designer with a new design firm. Your savvy prospects probably won't ask you to work on spec. Those who do will (most likely) understand your diplomatic refusal. Uninitiated (or possibly unscrupulous) clients need to be educated, but still turned down politely.

If you feel you must work on spec, keep your time to a bare minimum. Only submit basic ideas and simple sketches (no full-blown presentations or refined comps). Place your copyright notice on all visuals and date everything. Photocopy all graphics and paperwork. Now, dig up your old rabbit's foot for luck — you may need some!

hourly rate of $47.95, you end up with 12.51 or about 12½ hours to spend on this job. In other words, you will need to limit yourself to 12½ hours in order to be adequately compensated for your work.

Now let's go back to what the perceived value of your work is. Is $1,500 a fair price and a competitive rate in your area for a four-page, 11-by-17-inch four-color brochure? This is where your instincts, experience and assessment of the market value of your work come into play. Research and regard the so-called going rates care-

Lowballing

It's safe to say that at the beginning of your career you won't be commanding the fees of an established studio. Oh, there's nothing to stop you from quoting high prices, but without a proven track record, you're going to be unhappy. You'll have to price competitively. Sometimes—at first, and maybe often—this means lowballing a bid to get a job. I talked to many designers who still use this strategy to get a particularly valuable assignment. This is not a mistake, nor does it reflect the fall of the high and mighty—it's just business. These designers, with years of experience, an overflow of clientele and lucrative fees, are looking at the big picture and thinking in the long term. Clients may choose you simply because you're new and a good buy. So don't think "cheap," think "reasonably priced." Don't say "discounts," say "negotiation."

At the last studio where we worked, we did our own estimates and billing, we were familiar with what the going rate was in the market place for various kinds of projects. People expected a struggling young firm to be a little more negotiable, and we were. We knew what the major studios were charging and tried to come in a little bit under that. Some of our first clients were people shopping for a good price.

Don Sibley, Sibley/Peteet Design

fully. If your fees are strictly bargain basement, smart buyers may equate this with poor quality product. Conversely, inflated pricing will lose you a job just as easily ("You're way too expensive and just not worth it. I can get it cheaper down the street!"). An honest price that reflects market value—whether it's the high or low bid—is always the best stratagem.

Charging by the Task

So your average hourly rate should also factor in what you think the going rate is for different design tasks. *The Graphic Artists Guild Handbook: Pricing & Ethical Guidelines* (distributed by North Light Books) gives rates and billing procedures that are customary for professionals in the graphic arts. Average billable hourly rates are broken down as follows for graphic designers:

- Principal - $125 per hour
- Project designer - $100 per hour
- Junior designers - $75 per hour
- Production - $50 per hour

Obviously, a job demanding a lot of production, and very little design, will yield a lower price (based on the perceived value of the expertise going into it) than one that requires the skills of an experienced designer and production manager.

When determining what to

charge, don't forget that you're a start-up business. The figures quoted above represent an average that includes studios and agencies that have been in business for years. Factor in your experience and your reputation when determining what your fees should be. If you've figured that you need to charge $47.95 per hour to cover expenses and turn a profit, establish a range where you bill $40 per hour for production and clerical time and $60 per hour for design time. (Creative time, including client meetings and concept development, is generally billed at a rate of about one-third over the fee charged for production.)

One final note: When talking to a client about fees and expenses, refer to the project "budget," not "what it will cost" or "the money involved." If they seem reluctant to talk about what they expect to spend, explain to them that it's done for their benefit to let you know what they've been allocated or are able to afford.

Freebies

Low prices are not forever when your work is good and your services are in demand. However, you need to build up a portfolio, and in order to do this, you must initially look at the scope of the assignment rather than the figure on your invoice. And you will want to do pro bono work as well. Killer design jobs that yield great looking sam-

ples and/or prestige are excellent self-promotion vehicles and valuable bargaining chips for your design future.

Civic, health or arts organizations frequently cannot pay very much but often offer exciting creative opportunities and fabulous exposure. These "little" jobs are also fun and satisfying. Nonpaying only in regard to your pocketbook, pro bono assignments can be stimulating design challenges and wonderful reputation builders. When working with these groups it's OK to ask about being reimbursed for out-of-pocket expenses or negotiating a trade-off in services. You'll find out more in chapter seven about the promotional value of pro bono work.

Step 2: Preparing and Presenting a Proposal

Keep in mind that unless you get the job and can bill your client for your time, every written proposal costs you time. Although it's an essential part of doing business, writing a proposal is basically nonrevenue-producing work. You'll want to give every pitch your best shot, but don't overdo it—keep your time to a minimum.

Your proposal should say, "This is me. Here's what I have to offer. You're special. I've got a solution to your unique problem. Here's how I can meet your needs."

Your proposal will also be the means by which your clients compare your costs and concepts with that of your competition. It stands to reason then that a good proposal is crucial. The components of a well-written proposal should include:

• **Introduction:** This reiterates the sequence of events so far and what you've discussed with your client, "As you remember. . . . As we discussed. . . ."

• **Analysis:** This shows that you have listened to what the client has said. You've looked at the problem, studied their market and investigated the competition. Now, present this research as facts and figures. Tailor your analysis to this individual client's special situation and design needs.

• **Creative process:** Answers. What makes this job a singular design challenge? How will your concept solve the problem as outlined?

• **Production process:** How will the bright idea be guided into reality?

• **Fees, billing and timetable:** Be specific, detailed, accurate and honest.

• **Your track record:** Back yourself with a résumé, client list, mission statement, or a statement of the philosophy behind your business. This may provide the final touch in convincing a client that you're the design firm to hire. Don't be afraid to blow your own horn.

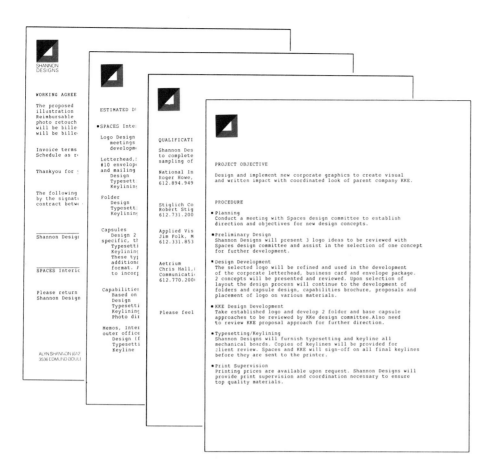

Proposals can vary in length and content depending on the client and the nature of the project. These proposals for different projects from Siebert Design Associates and Shannon Designs reflect your range of options for presenting this information. Both, however, have certain key features in common. They detail what services the designer will provide, what those services will cost, what expenses will be reimbursed to the designer, how costs for client changes will be handled, and include a request for the client's signature to acknowledge agreement with these costs for the work to commence.

REIMBURSABLE EXPENSES

Fees indicated on pag
These expenses are ty
and messenger service
calls). Estimates for
at final layout stage
invoice at cost with

MATERIALS TO BE PROVI

The client shall prov
All copy provided sha
The client shall proc
production of artworł
conclusive as to the
prior to their releas

REVISIONS AND ADDITIO

Any revisions or addi
Agreement shall be ba
in any fixed fee or ç
additional services i
in the extent of worł
of the project, and ç
for a specific phase

OWNERSHIP

Drawings, final mecha
visual presentation r
Designer. All materi
designer unless other
have reasonable acces
review. Complete buyc

PAYMENT

Before we begin Phase
a retainer equal to ç
is due upon completic
due upon completion c

If this proposal is ø
and return one to us

_____
Accepted

SIEBERT DESIGN
PROPOSAL
_____

TO: DATE: / /
                                         PROJECT NO:
                                         NAME:

FROM: Siebert Design Associates, Inc.
      308 East 8th Street
      Cincinnati, Ohio 45202

OBJECTIVES
_____

SCOPE
_____

Phase 1, We shall review all existing communications and discuss
         design direction.

Phase 2, We shall present for your approval, three design
         concepts in 1/2 scale sketch form.

Phase 3, We shall refine the concepts in the form of one tight
         comp and prepare camera-ready artwork and printing
         specifications.

Phase 4, We shall supervise printing to ensure quality and prompt
         delivery

COMPENSATION
_____

Fees shall be billed on an hourly basis and will not exceed
a guaranteed maximum fee for the following phases:

PHASE 1: Review and research...................... $

PHASE 2: Design Development........................$

PHASE 3: Refinement and production.................$

PHASE 4: Print supervision.........................$

_____
TOTAL..$

Sometimes it's extremely difficult to get the client to tell you precisely how much they want to spend until after you put a proposal in front of them. Then, somehow, they magically know exactly how much they can afford.

Rex Peteet, Sibley/Peteet Design

Present the proposal in person. One-on-one, face-to-face is the best way to immediately meet the issues and to address any questions. After all, a written proposal is merely words and numbers on paper, and your reputation is only a lofty intangible. You, in the flesh, are another matter. A personal presentation shows your commitment to the project, to the team, and it is a dramatic demonstration of who you are and what you can do. You care enough to be there right from the beginning, and you'll be there all the way. You can solve the problem; you're there to say: "I'm here to give you the answer!"

By the same token, if the proposal must be mailed or delivered, follow up immediately to make sure this valuable package arrived safely and to avail yourself for discussion.

Lastly, try to close the sale. Strike while the iron is hot at the end of the personal presentation. If the proposal is mailed, target a confirmation/award date.

Estimating Costs

Coming up with a budget for a job isn't too difficult once you've determined what tasks need to be done. Assuming that you have an hourly billing rate for the tasks involved, estimate the amount of time involved in performing each task. If you charge $30 per hour for production time and you estimate a job will take five hours to paste-up, multiply $30 by 5 to come up with an estimate of $150 for paste-up. Use the same task list that served as your scheduling guide and do this for all tasks involved in your project. Don't forget to figure in charges for your consultation time in meetings with clients, vendors and other suppliers.

A design job, even a small assignment, is a bit like a ride on the Orient Express for your client. He or she has a vague notion of how the train works, but doesn't really understand how to make it go, or how to get to the destination safely, on time and at the stated fare. They are hoping to get to their destination with personal service and tender care. Now think of a runaway train going incredibly fast and out of control, arriving who knows where or when or in what condition. The crash of a runaway train is an apt metaphor when you consider that a botched job with an errant budget will lead to the wreck of a business relationship. But the design process can be a splendid trip—an edifying journey for both you and your client (and another feather in the engineer's cap). No unpleasant surprises and no unhappy conclusion. Figuring costs and keeping track of expenses to stay on budget is the way to keep things running smoothly (see page 51 for a sample budget sheet).

Step 3: Get It In Writing

A handshake is a fine token of trust and cooperation, but this gesture provides no real information and is hardly legal proof of any transaction. Once your proposal has been accepted, it's important to establish with your client what the breakdown of expenses (compensation for time and reimbursable costs) on a project will be, and how it will be billed.

Both clients and designers should be well aware of the absolute necessity for some sort of written documentation at the outset of a project. You needn't fear or loathe this paperwork. What you

YOUNGBLOOD, SWEAT & TEARS

PHASE I/CREATIVE ESTIMATE

CLIENT

JOB DESCRIPTION

JOB NUMBER

DATE

CONCEPT DEVELOPMENT FEE

SUPPLIES/MATERIALS

SHIPPING/COURIER

TOTAL

INCLUDES INITIAL PRESENTATION

CLIENT SIGNATURE IS REQUIRED

SUBMITTED BY

DATE SUBMITTED

APPROVED BY

DATE APPROVED

ONE BUCKHEAD PLAZA

YOUNGBLOOD, SWEAT & TEARS

PHASE II/PRODUCTION
ESTIMATE

CLIENT

JOB DESCRIPTION

JOB NUMBER

DATE   ESTIMATE NUMBER

PRODUCTION & SUPERVISION FEE	$
COPYWRITING	$
TYPOGRAPHY	$
PHOTO STATS	$
PHOTOGRAPHY	$
ILLUSTRATION	$
RETOUCH/PRINTS	$
ENGRAVING	$
PRINTING	$
SUPPLIES/MATERIALS	$
SHIPPING/COURIER	$
TOTAL	$

THESE ESTIMATES MAY VARY 15%. THE ABOVE PRICES ARE BASED ON NORMAL SCHEDULES, UNLESS OTHERWISE STATED. PRICES QUOTED ARE VALID 30 DAYS FROM DATE OF ESTIMATE. IF THERE IS A PRICE CHANGE AT THE TIME OF ACTUAL PRODUCTION, A REVISED ESTIMATE WILL BE ISSUED.

CLIENT SIGNATURE IS REQUIRED BEFORE AGENCY CAN PROCEED.

SUBMITTED BY

DATE SUBMITTED

APPROVED BY

DATE APPROVED

ONE BUCKHEAD PLAZA 3060 PEACHTREE ROAD SUITE 510 ATLANTA GEORGIA 30305 404/237 7722 FAX 404/237 8806

An estimate may be part of a proposal or may be presented separately. The Youngblood, Sweat & Tears estimate breaks the project into stages and itemizes outside costs at the end. The document states that the estimate is valid for only 30 days, after which the charges may change. This protects the firm from having to eat increased costs if a client delays responding long enough that vendors and suppliers may have changed their prices.

DATE	DELIVERY DATE	□ ESTIMATE
ASSIGNMENT DESCRIPTION	(PREDICATED ON RECEIPT OF ALL MATERIALS TO BE SUPPLIED BY CLIENT)	□ ASSIGNMENT CONFIRMATION
	MATERIALS SUPPLIED BY	□ INVOICE
	FEE	
	ADVANCE	
TO	ASSIGNMENT NUMBER	
	CLIENT'S PURCHASE ORDER NUMBER	
	COMMISSIONED BY	
	TELEPHONE	

ITEMIZED EXPENSES. CLIENT SHALL REIMBURSE DESIGNER FOR ALL EXPENSES. IF THIS IS AN ESTIMATE OR ASSIGNMENT CONFIRMATION, ANY EXPENSE AMOUNTS ARE ESTIMATES ONLY. IF THIS IS AN INVOICE, EXPENSE AMOUNTS ARE FINAL.

CONSULTATION	
LAYOUT DESIGN	
PASTEUP MECHANICALS	
WRITING EDITING	
PROOFING RESEARCH	
TYPESETTING	
ILLUSTRATION PHOTOGRAPHY	
MATERIALS AND SUPPLIES	
PHOTOGRAPHIC REPRODUCTION	
STATS	
PRINTING	
TOLL TELEPHONES	
TRANSPORTATION AND TRAVEL	
SHIPPING AND INSURANCE	
OTHER	
	SUBTOTAL
	EXPENSES SUBTOTAL
ADVANCE	TOTAL DUE

ANY USAGE RIGHTS NOT EXCLUSIVELY TRANSFERRED ARE RESERVED TO DESIGNER. USAGE BEYOND THAT GRANTED TO CLIENT HEREIN SHALL REQUIRE PAYMENT OF A MUTUALLY AGREED UPON ADDITIONAL FEE SUBJECT TO ALL TERMS ON REVERSE.

Award
DESIGN

P.O. Box 82222
Fairbanks, AK 99708
(907) 455-6691

This two-part carbonless form can serve as Award Design's estimate, assignment confirmation or invoice when the appropriate box is checked. A printed statement tells the client that any itemized charges are only estimates unless this is an invoice.

want to write is a short instrument that clearly and simply spells out intent, a documentation of who buys what from whom for how much and when payment is due.

The Written Agreement

A written agreement or contract is a legal promise. It's the document that defines the all-important relationship between you and your client. As movie mogul Samuel Goldwyn used to say, "A verbal agreement isn't worth the paper it's printed on." The wording of any contract should be clean, clear and complete, and the document should be drafted in contemporary language — archaic Latin buzz words or bombastic legalese don't validate a thing. Information should be accurate and language must be explicit, leaving no possibility for inference or assumption.

A simple letter agreement works for many designers who delineate their terms and payment schedule on small jobs in this way. A formal contract on a store-bought form is OK, but it may not give you the leeway to customize terms for individual clients or to address special situations. This approach may also be too "cookie cutter" for clients who rightly demand individual attention and may wonder why you, as a designer, didn't bother to design your own forms. It's better to go with custom contracts built off a template of your basic terms and conditions and tailored to the client's project. These agreements are easily generated on even the most Spartan computers.

The Elements of a Written Agreement
Your written agreement should clearly define for all concerned:

- The project and its scope;
- Responsibilities — what the design firm does and what the client does;
- What services will be performed;
- When these services will be performed and how long it will take;
- What it will cost for these services;
- Who pays for what;
- How and when payment will be made, stating that fees and expenses will be billed on an itemized invoice;
- What constitutes extra work (corrections, additions and alterations) and how additional work will be compensated; and
- Protections for both parties (rights and copyrights).

You'll find more information on contracts in *The Graphic Artists Guild Handbook: Pricing & Ethical Guidelines*, and Tad Crawford's *Business and Legal Forms for Graphic Designers* (Allworth Press, distributed by North Light Books) includes information on contracts as well as contract samples.

Letters of Agreement

One way to draft an agreement between yourself and a client is to divide your exchange into two distinct documents: 1) the general contract delineating your working arrangement, and 2) the letter of agreement outlining the particulars on a specific job.

Before you draft anything, discuss all particulars and negotiate terms (except price, which you will stipulate in writing). Once you and your client are in accord, send the general contract as a written confirmation of what was discussed. This is an outline of the basic provisions that you and your client have worked out. Send this contract at the outset of your relationship, thus contracts are sent only once and redundant paperwork with later assignments is avoided. Then before you begin work on an assignment, send a letter of agreement for the client to sign and return as a confirmation of the details outlined in your contract. Also stipulate that all other work will be covered by additional letters of agreement. Get the document signed, returned and filed. (Of course, both parties should sign and file individual copies of all paperwork.)

Finally, remember that contracts and written agreements are merely pieces of paper. A signature doesn't insure performance or payment. What actually makes for a solid deal are the people who sign on the dotted line. And while reaching an

Agreement between
Shapiro Design Associates Inc. ("SDA")
141 Fifth Avenue
New York, NY 10010

and

XYZ Corporation, Inc. ("XYZ")
123 Any Avenue
Your Town, USA 00000

_by:_ _____
for XYZ

_____
Date

_____
Signature

_____
Title

1 General Working Agreement
This letter defines the terms and conditions of our working relationship. All projects or services that SDA may be contracted to produce or provide for XYZ will be subject to the following:

2 Working/Billing Phases
Based on our experience with long-term communications projects, we have found it mutually advantageous to handle each project in logical working/billing phases.
Concept revisions, extensive alterations, or a switch in marketing objectives sometimes make it impossible to accurately estimate in advance the total cost of a project. Planning the work, cost estimating and billing in several phases permits SDA or XYZ to adjust for such revisions and/or halt work before completion if a project is postponed or cancelled.
Any cancelled project is billed only through phases and/or portions of phases that were actually completed by SDA.
For each project, XYZ will receive a Proposal/Estimate outlining the project specifications and our proposed scope of services and working/billing phases. Each Proposal/Estimate will contain a project budget, which includes estimated fees for professional services and separate itemized costs for anticipated out-of-pocket expenses.
We will begin work upon XYZ's approval of the Proposal/Estimate; your approval (written or oral) will constitute an agreement between us.

3 Payment
XYZ agrees to pay SDA in accordance with the terms specified in each Proposal/Estimate. On new or larger projects, retainers are required before we begin work.
Unless otherwise specified, all subsequent payments

are due within thirty (30) days of the invoice date.
If you have any questions regarding an invoice, you must contact us upon receipt. If billing questions or possible errors are not reported to us within ten (10) days, the invoice is payable as written. Statements are sent to clients on a monthly basis. Interest on past due balances is charged at the rate of 18 percent per annum or 1 1/2 percent per month.
We reserve the right to refuse completion or delivery of work until past due balances are paid.

4 Out-of-Pocket Expenses
Fees for professional services do not include outside purchases, such as (but not limited to) printing, typography, linotronic outputs, photography, retouching, color separations, photostats, illustrations, art and color proofing materials, shipping and messengers.
Expenses are itemized on each invoice. The standard agency service charge of 17.65% is included in the price you are billed. Expenses are subject to applicable New York or New Jersey sales taxes unless: **1)** you are a non-profit organization; **2)** the work is for resale and you have submitted a resale certificate; or **3)** the work is done for and billed to offices outside the states of New York or New Jersey.
If consultation or supervisory services are required in out-of-town locations, we will bill lodging, meals and transportation at cost. Reimbursement for mileage is calculated at current allowable rates.

5 Revisions and Alterations
New work requested by XYZ and performed by SDA after a Proposal/Estimate has been approved is considered a revision or alteration. If the job changes to an extent that substantially alters the specifications described in the original estimate, we will submit a proposal revision memo to you, and a revised or additional fee must be agreed by both parties before further work proceeds.
Author's Alterations (AAs) and other copy changes requested after approved layouts or mechanicals are completed are billed at hourly rates as follows:
Principal $00   per hour
Senior Designer   00
Mechanical Artist   00
Assistant   00
In-house Typesetting 00
These rates will be in effect until December 31, 1991.

6 Overtime
Estimates are based on a reasonable time schedule, and may have to be revised to take into consideration your "rush" requests requiring overtime or weekends. Knowledge of your deadline is essential to provide an accurate estimate. In addition, outside suppliers such as photostat houses often charge a 100% to 200% mark-up on overtime after 5:00 p.m. or on weekends.

7 Nature of Copy
XYZ agrees to exercise due diligence in its direction to us regarding preparation of materials, and must be able to substantiate all claims and representations. You are responsible for all trademark, service mark, copyright and

patent infringement clearances. You are also responsible for arranging, prior to publication, any necessary legal clearance of material we prepare.
Upon XYZ's written request and at your expense, we will affix a copyright notice to the work and register the copyright to obtain protection under the Copyright Act of 1976.

8 Errors and Omissions
It is XYZ's responsibility to check proofs carefully for accuracy in all respects, ranging from spelling to technical illustrations. SDA is not liable for errors or omissions. Your signature or that of your authorized representative is required on all mechanicals or art work prior to release for printing or other implementation.

9 Placement of Advertising
At your request, we will purchase media space on your behalf through our Print Media Inc. division. Space will be billed to you at current published rates, which include the standard agency commission.

10 Inspection of Books
Upon reasonable notice, any and all invoices from our vendors, time sheets and other documentation relating to your account will be available to you.
Inspection at our office by your authorized representative may be arranged during usual business hours.

11 Property and Suppliers' Performance
SDA will take all reasonable precautions to safeguard the property you entrust to us. In the absence of negligence on our part; however, we are not responsible for loss, destruction, damage or unauthorized use by others of such property. We will use our best efforts to ensure quality and timely delivery of all printed, (silkscreened, engraved, or otherwise reproduced) pieces. Although we will use our best efforts to guard against any loss to you through failure of our vendors, media or others to perform in accordance with their commitments, SDA is not responsible for failure on their part.
If you select your own vendors, other than those recommended by us, you may request that we coordinate their work. If at all possible, we will attempt to do so, but cannot in any way be held responsible for quality, price, performance or delivery.

12 Rights of Ownership
Once a project has been delivered by us and is fully paid for by XYZ, SDA will assign the reproduction rights of the design for the use(s) described in the proposal.
According to the Copyright Law of 1976, the rights to all design and art work, including but not limited to photography and/or illustration created by independent photographers or illustrators retained by SDA or purchased from a stock agency on your behalf, remain with the individual designer, artist, photographer or illustrator. Unless a purchase of "all rights" (a "buyout") is negotiated with SDA and/or with the photographer, illustrator, stock agency or his/her authorized representative, you may not use or reproduce the design or the images therein for a purpose other than the one(s) initially stipulated. If you

wish to use a design we have created and/or the images within it for another purpose or project, including a reprint or exhibition, you must contact us to arrange the transfer of rights and any additional fees before proceeding.
If printing or other implementation is done through your vendors, you agree to return to us all our original mechanicals and art work (slides, prints, drawings, etc.) within two weeks, and to provide us with 25 printed samples of each project.
We reserve the right to photograph and/or distribute or publish for our firm's promotional and marketing needs any work we create for you, including mock-ups and comprehensive presentations, as samples for our portfolio, firm newsletter, brochures, slide presentations, and other similar media.
We agree to store mechanical boards and computer disks for a period of two years beyond delivery of a job. Thereupon, we reserve the right to discard them.

13 Term and Termination
The term of this agreement will continue until terminated by either of us upon thirty (30) days written notice.
If you should direct us at any time to cancel, terminate or "put on hold" any previously authorized purchase or project, we will promptly do so, provided you hold us harmless for any cost incurred as a result.
Upon termination of this agreement, SDA will transfer to XYZ all your property and materials in our control and for which you have paid.
XYZ will indemnify and hold SDA harmless for any loss or expense (including attorney's fees), and agree to defend SDA in a threatened or actual suit, claim or action arising in any way from our working relationship. This includes, but is not limited to assertions made against XYZ and any of its products or services arising from the publication of materials that we prepare and you approve before publication.

14 Additional Provisions
The validity and enforceability of this agreement will be interpreted in accordance with the laws of the State of New York applicable to agreements entered into and performed within the State of New York.
This agreement is our entire understanding and may not be modified in any respect except by an executed agreement.
If we must retain attorneys to collect our invoices, we will be entitled to reasonable attorney's fees, court costs, and interest at the maximum rate permitted by law.

Shapiro Design Associates Inc.

_____
Ellen Shapiro

SHANNON
DESIGNS

Initial Meeting(s) and Research		$ 480.00
2 Rough Layout Ideas		960.00
1 Final Comprehensive layout		525.00
Art/Prints for presentation		250.00
Photography (Film and Processing)		1500.00
Art Direction at Photo Session		250.00
Typesetting for 3 Boxes		500.00
Keylining for 3 Boxes		600.00

Printing

	QTY	PRICE
3 Boxes, die cut, score, fold and glue,	1,000	$2,598.00
.018 SDS stock, 4 color with varnish	5,000	5,092.00
	10,000	7,848.00
(each of 3)	15,000	9,980.00
	25,000	13,860.00
Prep and Filmwork based on 3 8x10 seps bleeds 4 sides, reverses and tints		$2,260.00

Reimbursable expenses such as but not limited to messenger services, photo retouching or client alterations will be billed in addition to the above fees. Alterations to final mechanical will be billed at $60.00 per hour.

Invoice terms are $2500 down prepayment and balance on delivery.

WORKING AGREEMENT
The above proposal has been reviewed and is accepted as evidenced by the signatures below. This working agreement will serve as a binding contract between Shannon Designs and Management Software Inc.

Alyn Shannon 10/31/88   _____
Shannon Designs   Management Software Inc.

Please return signed copy of agreement and P.O. if required along with prepayment to Shannon Designs.

ALYN SHANNON (612) 722-2841
3536 EDMUND BOULEVARD, MPLS, MN 55406

When working with a client you know well, a simple working agreement added to the proposal, like this one from Shannon Designs (left), may be all the written agreement you'll need. With all first-time clients or when taking on big projects, you'll need something more formal and detailed like this agreement used by Shapiro Design Associates (above).

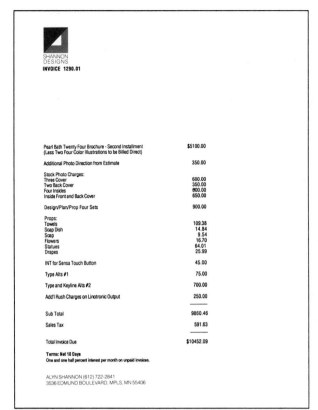

You can type up or print out your invoice on your letterhead as shown in this sample from Shannon Designs, assigning an invoice number to each. Or you can invest in some preprinted forms like Art Direction Inc.'s continuous forms. No matter how you create your forms, be sure your terms for payment are clearly printed on them. If you charge interest on overdue balances as Shannon does (1½ percent per month), you must state that clearly on the form, too.

agreement is often easier said than done, if you work with honest, ethical and reasonable folks (like yourself) you should have no problem.

Billing Procedures and Payment Schedules

Being charged by the hour, regardless of whether the rate is fair or the time reasonable, scares most folks half to death. (Remember when the plumber came to fix that pipe in your attic?) But a flat fee allows too much room for abuse of your time, responsibilities and energies. The client wants to get his money's worth, so you may be asked to jump hoops as a result. Complica-

Sales Tax

Many start-up businesses often ignore charging (and then actually remitting) sales tax. Let's clarify: You don't pay sales tax — your client does. It is your responsibility to collect sales tax for the state at designated intervals. If the state discovers that you should have collected, but did not, you will be liable for this tax plus penalties. They will catch up with you, so the best advice is to keep squeaky clean with your state's agency and requirements.

tions can play havoc with your schedule so you underestimate the workload or costs involved. Here's a good alternative: Estimate or quote the job at a specific price, billed in phases. Detail each phase explicitly and specify that extra work not covered in the agreement will be charged to the client as an additional expense at your hourly rate. You may also want to bill by completion of phases or consider installments based on a different criterion. The following are some payment schedules to consider:

• **Payment in Thirds:** Many designers make it a standard practice to ask for one-third of the total fee for a job upon agreement, one-

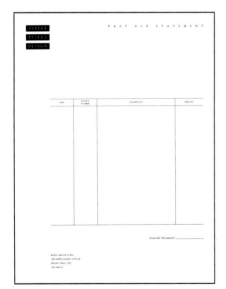

Never let an unpaid invoice just slide by. Send clients a past due statement each month to remind them to pay you. This two-part carbonless form used by Sibley/Peteet Design has columns for the invoice number, a description of the project or item involved and the amount due.

third upon approval of comprehensives, and the remainder within 30 days of delivery of mechanicals or printed pieces.

• **Payment in Halves:** If the job you are working on is larger in scope, you may consider asking for one-half of the fee upon agreement and the rest in scheduled installments or monthly payments.

• **Payment in Full First:** For smaller jobs, get your fee in cash up front.

Finally, many designers also recommend giving totals when invoicing clients rather than itemizing the number of hours and their billing rate. Although you should let your clients know up front what you charge for your time, there's no need to raise your clients' curiosity about why they were charged a given rate for a particular task.

Step 4: Getting Your Money

New clients can be big risks as well as great opportunities. There's always the chance that any of your customers may be slow to pay or may not pay at all. Exercise a bit of caution to save yourself some time, energy and money. Make the following policies part of your standard procedure in dealings with clients, and you're less likely to get burned:

• **Get everything in writing.** Have your client sign all agreements and sign off on any correspondence or documentation.

• **Be informed.** Get all financial particulars, including the name of a new client's bank and the account number, by having him or her fill out a standard credit application (generic forms can be found at your office supply store).

• **Investigate three or four credit references** that your client has supplied to you or consult the Better Business Bureau. The size of a savings or checking account is no guarantee that you will ever see that money. Remember, you want to check history, not security. This kind of checking would be unnecessary with a client like Procter & Gamble or *Time* magazine, but do investigate as appropriate.

• **Get a personal guarantee of payment** from the owner, not the corporation.

• **Don't finance your client's job.** The fees for your professional services don't include outside purchases (called out-of-pocket expenses). Itemize these expenses and add a service charge to the bill (generally 15 to 20 percent). You can also stipulate that outside purchases such as printing and photography will be billed directly to the client (or request a retainer so that you have cash up front to pay these vendors).

Steps to Avoid Getting Stiffed

You've stipulated your billing policy in a written agreement with your client. It should state when payment is due for services rendered. Now you need to bill and receive payment at each stage of the agreed payment schedule prior to proceeding to the next stage.

Before any unpleasantness occurs, make sure all the terms of your agreement are perfectly clear. Take a job only when you are certain both parties know when (and how) payment is due.

But what do you do about slow-paying or nonpaying clients? Here are a few words of advice for dealing with deadbeats. (You may label these characters a little more colorfully if you prefer.) Leonard Bendell, author of *Payment in Full* (Triad Publishing), offers these suggestions for successfully getting what's due:

- Invoice when the work is delivered with the term "net 30 days."
- If you're not paid within 14 days, remind the client with a second statement.
- The bill is overdue if not received within 40 days.
- At the 40-day point, ask why you haven't been paid.
- Find out when you can expect payment, or state when you expect payment, but don't threaten.
- Be reasonable, understanding, but resolute. Offer an alternative payment plan (for example, weekly installments over three months).

My three largest jobs were for clients who seemed respectable and responsible. I was very excited about the work I was producing for them. I put in a lot of overtime on the weekends and evenings to get the jobs finished by their deadline. The only deadline that wasn't met was their deadline to pay me for the work.

Adela Ward Batin, Award Design and Alaska Angler Publications

- Don't harass. There are laws, such as the Fair Debt Collection Practices Act, that govern collection methods.
- Send more letters or make intermittent phone calls until you're paid or the bill is 75 days overdue. If the account has not been settled at this point, you could sue in small claims court or hire a collection agency. (However, agencies usually keep about half of what they collect.) Or you may decide to cut your losses if you now feel getting any money from the client is unrealistic.

Contract Fulfillment

Get a lawyer if you have a legal problem, contract question or dispute with a client. I personally know one artist with a law degree, but he is a most definite exception to the rule. Even if you consider yourself to be the Perry Mason of the design world, a little legal ad-

vice can only help. Should push come to shove, you might be able to navigate somewhat painlessly through a minor altercation (which includes settling privately out of court), but get a lawyer for cases outside of small claims court.

As defined in the *Graphic Artists Guild Handbook: Pricing and Ethical Guidelines* (distributed by North Light Books), "small claims courts give access to the legal system while avoiding the usual encumbrance, costs and lengthy duration of formal courts . . . (the) procedure is streamlined, speedy and available for a minimal fee. Artists can handle their own cases with a little preparation." If you must go the legal route—and the sum of money concerned is small—a small claims procedure is a way to get your day in court. Consult your city's clerk of courts or the Better Business Bureau for more information and guidelines.

Rex Peteet & Don Sibley

Establishing a Fair Price

Rex Peteet and Don Sibley shared approximately eight years of similar staff experiences before venturing out on their own in 1982. They attended the same college (and even had an art class together), but they were only acquaintances during their school days. Both worked at advertising agencies and various studios after leaving school, but didn't develop a friendship until their last stop as staff designers for the same firm.

It was largely professional timing that prompted Sibley and Peteet to form a partnership and go out on their own. "We were the senior people at the studio," observes Sibley. "We had direct client contact and were basically functioning as business principals without any kind of title. We realized that we felt competent in our ability to do it on our own." And by that time, the partners had developed a strong friendship and similar professional goals. "Our philosophy toward design and similarities in lifestyles were so compatible," he says, "we felt this would be the perfect partnership."

Well rooted in the Dallas community, Sibley and Peteet parlayed their many contacts among clients, vendors and friends into a strong client base. "We also went after a lot of arts organizations that

needed pro bono work," says Peteet. "This gave us an opportunity to be associated with very reputable organizations, give something back to the community, and be able to get a credit line. We weren't concerned with making a lot of money. We just wanted to survive and do the best work we could—the kind of work that would get us into shows and would get us some visibility."

Having exercised much control while managing projects in their staff positions, Sibley and Peteet had a fairly good idea of how to charge for their time. "We did our own estimates and billing," says Sibley. "We were familiar with what the going rate was in the market place for various kinds of projects."

However, he points out that at the onset, clients expected them to negotiate their prices a bit. "People expected a struggling young firm to be a little more negotiable," he observes. "And we were. We knew what the major studios were charging and tried to come in a little bit under that. Some of our first clients were people shopping for a good price. Starting out you have to make yourself attractive," he says. "If you're not a proven entity yet, people are not going to be willing to pay as much as they would for a proven studio."

The bargain philosophy worked for Sibley/Peteet, but Sibley points

out that through the years the firm has brought its prices up to the current market rate. "You can't charge low prices forever," Peteet adds. "But if you're smart and you've kept your studio small and your overhead low, you can afford to bid low at the beginning [to establish yourself]. As you get better, have more work to show and your studio gets larger, you have to let your prices come up accordingly."

The partners also found it more realistic, and agreeable to their clients, to price their work on a project-by-project basis. Indeed, they estimate that about 90 percent of their work was billed out that way. Sibley and Peteet have a unique way of breaking down their billing time on a project into three segments. "We build in a concept fee," points out Peteet. "A concept fee is a way to separate the thinking from the rest of the job. The concept fee has a range, depending on how many designers are involved. If it's one or two designers, obviously we can afford to do it for much less than if the entire studio is working on it."

Next comes an estimate for refining a concept. They then arrive at another estimate for application—the actual production of a job—once there is an agreement about the design concept. Says Sibley, "The concept and refinement estimates cover the thinking of anywhere from two to eight people, depending on the client and what they can afford. All prices are based on the history of the market. In many cases, we're bidding against other studios, so this keeps us all pretty honest."

Sibley/Peteet generally prefer to get half of a project's estimated price up front, as soon as the job is awarded. The remainder of a project is billed out in quarters, or the last half billed at completion. Occasionally, on some long-term proj-ects, the firm has billed on a monthly basis.

The designers believe that a job's paperwork is crucial, but as Peteet confesses, "We haven't had a contract in every situation. Again, because we've gotten into these long-term relationships where nothing is signed, almost like a gentlemen's agreement — that's just the way it is. However, I would never recommend that for some-body just starting out. There are too many lowlifes out there that will take advantage of a start-up de-sign firm.

"I think you develop a sixth sense about when it's not neces-sary. A lot of times it can be very cumbersome in a long-term rela-tionship — every time you turn around they have to sign some-thing. It can be awkward. But I think when you're starting out it's not inappropriate at all."

Through experience, Sibley and Peteet have learned how to sharpen their business acumen when it comes to establishing a fair price for their services. They point out that learning the pricing game takes some time. Eventually, experience makes bidding on jobs an easy pro-cess. "Whatever the market will bear will determine your price," summarizes Peteet. "It's not some-thing you're going to be able to do right away, but it's a skill you de-velop — much like becoming a good designer. It's about feelings and senses. Sometimes you win and sometimes you lose."

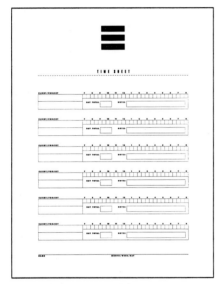

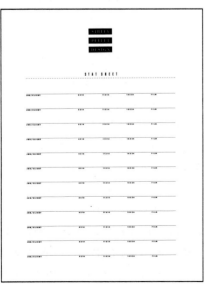

Sibley/Peteet Design uses these business forms to keep track of design and production time and expenses.

Preparing a Strong Proposal

"I feel like I've started my own design firm four times," says Ellen Shapiro, principal of Shapiro Design Associates in New York City. "The first time was in about 1974, when I started freelancing out of my apartment. I just wasn't prepared for the realities of the business world and got killed financially. In other words, clients didn't pay. After working a whole summer on one project — packaging and promotion for a product that ulti-

mately wasn't brought to market because the client went bankrupt — I took a full-time job for a communications firm. It may not have been the greatest career move, but it was safe, and safety was what I needed then," she admits.

"The second time was two years later when I met someone who seemed like the perfect partner. He had just left a well-known corporate identity firm. After looking at

each other's portfolios and talking for a couple of hours, we signed a partnership agreement and went into business right away, setting up shop as Design Concern," says Shapiro. But this firm lasted just two years. "We parted company over the usual partnership squabbles — power and money," she admits.

"After the partnership broke up, each of us had to pick up the pieces and start all over again. So in 1978 I incorporated as Shapiro Design Associates, Inc. As part of the division of Design Concern's assets I got the office lease, which by that time was a 1,500-square-foot loft space in midtown. I had no choice but to go out and sell design — and I did." For the next five years Shapiro Design Associates grew by 20 percent each year and by 1985 included eight full-time employees. "We built fairly spectacular new 4,200-square-foot offices on Fifth Avenue, which, with salaries and other costs, brought our operating expenses to over $50,000 a month. When things are going that well, you can't imagine them any other way," says Shapiro.

"Then came the stock market crash of October 1987. It hurt us a lot because many of our clients were in financial services." As a result of belt-tightening all around and the loss of smaller clients that were swallowed up in mergers and

acquisitions, Shapiro was forced to downsize. "By spring of 1988 I had to make drastic changes to keep the firm alive," she says. "One by one, my employees were let go or left; I sublet the offices to a company in the energy business, moved to a much smaller space in the building, and cut back on every possible cost. It was like starting the business for the fourth time, humbled and sobered."

Shapiro Design today is back in the black. It consists of Ellen Shapiro, one full-time assistant who is a talented recent design school graduate, and a bookkeeper who comes in once a week. Shapiro also uses freelancers as needed and is thinking about hiring a second, administrative, assistant. Almost all type is set in-house on the Macintosh, which Shapiro says is an invaluable tool that allows her to write, design and typeset in one seamless operation. "Luckily, I have a particular advantage in the marketplace — that I am a writer as well as a designer. So companies will come to me for complete project management, from concept development to copy to production supervision."

Besides integrated services and a hands-on approach, another of Shapiro's strengths is client relations. In fact she's written an excellent book on the subject, *Clients and Designers* (Watson-Guptill).

Shapiro's proposals clearly define the design services to be provided, describing them in enough detail for the client to know easily what will be done when. Expenses are itemized and the billing schedule set out. Work that is not described in the proposal such as client changes or extra presentations will be billed in addition to the expenses listed in the proposal.

The book features interviews with a range of clients who have worked successfully with designers across the country. "Clients are in the position of power," Shapiro tells us. "Some of them will ask you to work on spec or make you jump through hoops and prepare a series of elaborate proposals to get one job. Some don't even call back to respond after you've put in days of work on a proposal. One goal in doing the book was to provide role models for clients, to show how it's done right and why good design does indeed mean good business."

Shapiro maintains that it's easy for designers, especially young ones just starting out, to get abused by clients. "The word 'abused' is perhaps too strong," she says, "maybe 'taken advantage of' is more accurate. In any event, it took me years to learn how to say 'no.' It took me years to learn how to make sure a job doesn't get out of control because of the client's lack of experience. There are times when you have to be assertive, to say, 'It has to be done this way,' or 'We can't work any more unless you agree to a higher fee.'"

How does a beginning designer learn to say no? "The key is clear communication, fair negotiation and then written agreement," she says. "Getting everything down on paper is essential. There has to be a written proposal for every job, large or small. Define exactly what the job is, what your role will be — scope of services." Detail your fees and all out-of-pocket costs by phase, Shapiro recommends. Spell out what is not included, such as additional pages or author's alterations, and spell out the rights you are transferring to the client.

Shapiro advises that all projects be broken down by phases. "Let's say it's a capabilities brochure and your fee will be $12,000. The proposal could state that a retainer of $3,000 is due before beginning work; $3,000 will be billed upon acceptance of the comprehensive presentation (Phase I); $3,000 upon completion of the photography and other art (Phase II); and $3,000 upon delivery of mechanicals to the printer (Phase III).

Working this way protects both parties and lets them know where they stand at all times," she says. "If the client is dissatisfied or has a change of marketing plans, they can cancel and know they have to pay for the work that was actually completed. Working and billing in phases also ensures that the designer is paid as the job progresses so that cash flow is steady."

Should the proposal be lengthy? Shapiro says, "Not necessarily. It depends on the job. Is it a complex project for a new client? Then, of course, yes. Or is it a smaller job for a long-standing account? Then a one-page letter can do.

"You can use some of the same

verbiage for various clients," she adds, "but I find that a new proposal has to be developed for each project because no two jobs are alike in purpose and content. Assuming that the fees are in the same ballpark, when choosing among three or four design firms of equal quality, many clients will make a decision based on the quality of the proposal. The proposal is the place to demonstrate your understanding of and commitment to the project."

For Shapiro, perhaps four is the charm. This successful designer is where she is today because she knows how to get and serve clients appropriately.

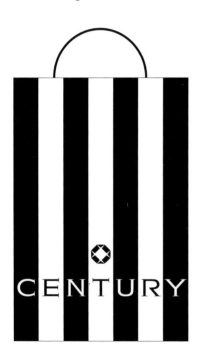

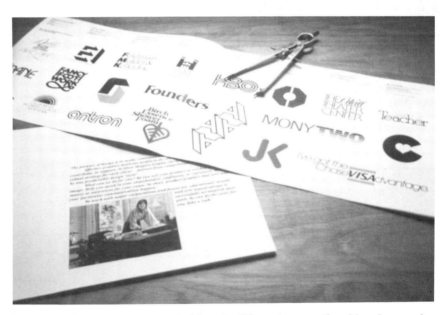

Throughout her career, represented here by this early promotional brochure and a recent project for Century Time Gems, one of Shapiro's great strengths has been her skill in handling client relations.

Adela Ward Batin

Make Sure You Get Paid in Full — and on Time

Adela Ward Batin, founder of Fairbanks, Alaska-based Award Design and Alaska Angler Publications, was frustrated with her isolation as a staff designer. "I had no contact with the client," she explains. "The contact person was the account ex-

ecutive. There was no way for me to get feedback directly from the client." Out of this frustration, and to satisfy her need for more professional and personal growth, Batin started her own studio in 1979. Award Design is now a successful, full-service advertising and graphic design business.

Her success with her own studio prompted Batin to start Alaska Angler Publications, a seven-year-old publishing firm that specializes in publications dealing with outdoor living and fishing in Alaska. In addi-

tion to book and magazine publishing, Alaska Angler Publications markets stock photos of Alaska and provides photo and editorial support to many national and regional magazines seeking material on Alaska.

Although Batin has attained many of her professional goals and is now able to respond more directly to her clients' needs, she nevertheless has cultivated a very keen instinct for balancing their expectations with her own professional needs — particularly when it comes to billing. "You need to make sure you bill your client for every minute you spend on a job," Batin says. "Always consider the bottom line. You can create the most beau-

tiful brochure or logo in the world, but if you don't get paid for it, you can't meet your obligations."

She also points out that it's important to keep track of time spent on a project. Batin uses a Daytimer journal for tracking job hours. "You may decide to cut back on a bill because you spent more time than you think it should have taken (or you overestimated the work involved). You may not have estimated correctly and the job took longer than you figured. In any event — for your own information as well as billing purposes — you need to know how much time you're spending on any given job."

Batin informs us that the way to avoid client disputes is to get an

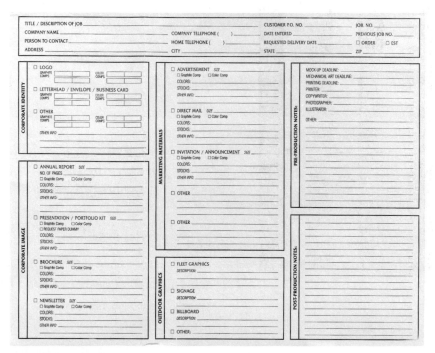

Job sheets like this one help keep Award Design's projects in order. The reverse side is a time sheet.

agreement on as many terms as possible up front and in writing. "You and the client need to agree on what the job is going to cost," she says. "I use an assignment confirmation form to get everything down on paper—what the job requires, when the deadline is and what the budget is."

She points out that establishing the price of a project with a client at the onset is especially important in Alaska, where, as Batin puts it, there is an appetite for "champagne on a beer budget. They want a four-color brochure designed and printed for $1,000. If you tell them it will cost more, they tell you that you're overpriced."

Batin also offers advice on getting paid. "Don't begin a large job with a new client unless you get a one-third or one-half deposit up front. And don't deliver the finished job until the client has paid you the balance due first." Batin has learned you can't always rely on your instincts when gauging a client's willingness and ability to fulfill financial obligations. "My three largest jobs were for clients who seemed respectable and responsible. I was very excited about the work I was producing for them," she says. "I put in a lot of overtime on the weekends and evenings to get the jobs finished by their deadline. The only deadline that wasn't met was their deadline to pay me for the work."

Batin learned that it's hard to

function as a project-generating designer if you encounter this situation too frequently in the early days of a business. "It takes a lot of creative energy out of you when you are stressed over not being paid, and try to figure out how to get your money back," observes Batin. "I had signed contracts. But one business went bankrupt. I was at the bottom of the list of creditors. They called us 'unsecured creditors.'

"I've learned that there are types of clients I don't want to work for," says Batin. "And I've learned that I can say 'no' to a job—even if it's the only offer I've had for a week. I'd rather spend eight hours working on my house than waste eight

This three-color brochure for the Fairbanks North Star Borough School District is typical of Batin's design and photography.

This book cover suggests the wide range of Batin's talents. She and her husband, Chris, wrote, designed, and published the book through their own publishing company, Alaska Angler Publications.

hours on a job for a client who did not pay for it because they didn't like it. Some people are hard to work with."

Batin has learned the hard way that finding a viable livelihood has a lot to do with finding clients who are amenable and fair as well as sincere in their intentions. "I prefer to pick and choose my clients. I do a much better job for the ones I get along with and who appreciate my talents."

CHAPTER 6

MANAGING YOUR NEW STUDIO

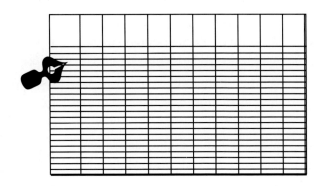

So you think you're organized? Got it together (if you could only remember where all the elements are)? Starting and running your own studio is very much like a juggling act. At times you'll feel as though you're juggling the task equivalents of a meat cleaver, bowling ball and cream pie. Just how many minor chores and major responsibilities can you keep in the air all at once? And make no mistake about it, you're going to be so busy, you may end up dropping a pin or two.

You know all the clichés: You're only one person. There are just so many hours in a day. You'll be wearing a lot of different hats. These homilies are timeworn, but (to throw in another antiquated phrase) right as rain.

Step 1: Managing Your Work

Managing your business and the projects you bring in is a matter of zeroing in on priorities. It's also a matter of keeping track of people, services, time and expenses. In order to manage effectively you will need to get organized, set up systems and procedures and maintain records and files on all aspects of your business.

Keeping Track of Projects

You must keep tabs on any project in order to stay on time. Graphic design often involves bringing to-gether many pieces to create a final, printed product. Making sure every component of a job is done, and done well, is imperative. As if keeping track of your end of a project isn't enough, you'll also need to watchdog the work being done by support services such as service bureaus and freelancers.

To keep a deadline and overall turnaround time in mind, break each project down into tasks and mini-tasks. After identifying each task and mini-task, assign an amount of time to each. From there you should be able to come up with a schedule and a completion date for each task. As each task is completed, record the date so you'll know exactly when it was done.

Create a job jacket for each project and place your schedule into the jacket or tack it on the outside. This way you will know at a glance what tasks still need to be completed on a given job, and whether or not the job is on schedule.

Some designers prefer to use a wall chart, a blackboard or bulletin board as a means of tracking progress of all ongoing projects. Regardless of your preferred method, or combination of methods, you'll need to keep track of (and come up with completion dates for) the following components or job phases. They are arranged here in approximate chronology of completion:

• **Conceptualization and roughs:** This is where you do your homework. You'll meet with the client, brainstorm, come up with a concept, and obtain the approval to schedule the other components that will go into successfully producing the final job.

• **Copy:** Schedule copy with client availability in mind for consultation, approval and brainstorming.

• **Photography:** Whether scheduling setup, location shots or selecting from client-furnished photography, you should factor in time for reviewing contact sheets and including the client in photo selection. Schedule time for retouching,

Theo Stephan uses this form to track projects going through Real Art Design Group. When a job comes in, the form is filled out with the names of those employees assigned to each stage of the project. Pertinent notes are written by the name. Even if you work alone, you might find a version of this sheet helpful for keeping tabs on, and notes about, the works in progress.

cropping and sizing.

- **Illustration:** Provide time for locating suitable talent, as well as plenty of time for roughs, revisions and final renderings.

- **Typesetting:** Whether typesetting on your computer or contracting type from a typehouse, schedule adequate time for copyfitting, proofreading and revisions.

- **Mechanicals:** Be sure to schedule time for client review and approval and possible revisions, as well as time for stats.

- **Color Separations/Films:** Schedule service bureau time if your printer doesn't take responsibility for this. If you're working on any job with a large quantity of four-color work, allow enough time for getting bids from several service bureaus. Remember also to schedule time for client approval of chromalins and Iris prints.

- **Printing:** Allow time to get quotes from several printers, time to review and obtain client approval on chromalins or color keys (if your printer handles this), as well as time to review bluelines and make any revisions. Factor in time to collate, trim, fold, stitch, die-cut or complete other processes involved in the job, in addition to including time for the actual print run. And don't forget to schedule press checks, possibly including the client in these checks, if the requirements for the job call for it.

Keeping the Client Posted

Nobody likes surprises. No matter how outstanding your design work may be, you will never be able to build a business if you do not have a reputation for developing good rapport. You'll need to communicate frequently and candidly with your clients and develop an understanding up front of what is required from each of you in order to bring about successful completion of a project. With every job you have an obligation to let your client know what you will be producing in the way of roughs and comps, when you will be producing them, and when he or she will be involved in the decision-making process. It is also your responsibility to schedule meetings and opportunities for client approval. It's crucial that you establish this with your client at the onset of a project so that you will be able to schedule client approval meetings at different stages of the job.

Some designers feel it is necessary to develop a history on each of their clients. In addition to a company's address, phone number(s) and contact information you may want to maintain a record of billing procedures, credit and financial information, plus any other information you deem pertinent to the business relationship. Any personal preferences or idiosyncrasies

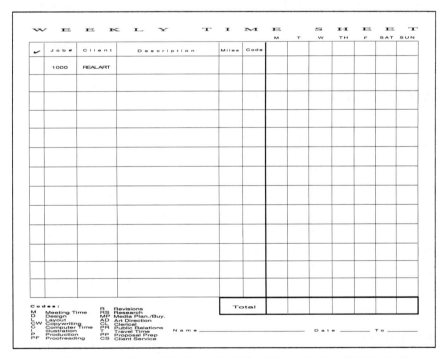

You should keep a weekly or daily time sheet, like this one for Real Art Design Group. It should detail what you did on each job you worked on, when you did it, and how long you spent doing it. This sheet will make it much easier for you to prepare invoices for clients and to estimate future jobs, because you'll know better how many hours you'll need to finish each phase of a project.

You may find it helpful to keep a job log like the one Theo Stephan uses. This sheet is ordered by job number and covers the major events in a job's life cycle: due date, date the job file was closed and stored, and the date the invoice was sent.

Job #	Date	Client	Description	Due Date	Date Closed	Invoice #	Invoice Date

Lori Siebert uses these job envelopes not only to record information about projects, but also to hold the smaller pieces of projects going through production at Siebert Design Associates.

can be kept track of in this file — particularly if your past experience with a client's projects has been fraught with a multitude of time-robbing revisions.

And remember, the cost of client revisions increase ten-fold with each stage of production. If it costs $10 to change something in a rough, it will cost $100 when it is typeset and pasted on a mechanical, and it will cost $1,000 to make the same change in the blueline stage. It's best to make revisions early on and establish a piece you and your client can agree upon at the beginning of a project.

Getting and Staying Organized

It's important to make a daily list of what needs to be done. At the end of the day you can make a list of tasks for the next day, taking note of tasks that need to be finished. Determine priorities by assigning a numerical value to each task. Make sure you tackle the tasks that have the highest priority on a given day.

Keep track of your ideas and what needs to be done. You can easily remind yourself about any aspect of a project, or about business in general, by recording it in a pocket notebook. If you can afford it and are enthralled with anything high tech, you could also record information on a pocket tape recorder. When you are back in your studio, transfer this information into a larger planning book. A calendar, diary or any scheduling log can help plan, schedule, and keep track of all projects, meetings and other business obligations. You'll find that by maintaining some sort of plan book, you'll be able to keep track of all aspects of your business on a day-to-day basis so nothing will fall through the cracks.

Job Files
We talked a little about job jackets earlier in this chapter. Your job jacket will serve as storage for all project-related notes and correspondence, as well as for scheduling and supplier information. Your job jackets can be organized and stored alphabetically in a file cabinet, while oversized mechanicals and other project-related art should be stored in flat files.

In addition to categorizing your projects alphabetically by client, assign a number for each project. For example, the Acme logo job would be Acme #1001, while Acme's stationery and business cards would be Acme #1002. By assigning each project an identifying number, you can easily keep track of the chronological order of each of Acme's projects. Use these codes, as well, for identifying charges that are to be billed directly to a project.

Step 2: Managing Your Money

Running a tab at your local bistro is one thing. Running a business and not keeping tabs on income and expenses is another. Being a free spirit may definitely be a creative boon, but become a button-down banker with your bucks. It's absolutely crucial to know what money is coming in, how much you have at any time, and where it's going. To do otherwise is simply bad business and could ultimately lead to financial suicide.

Your Accounts

In order to keep track of business income and expenses, it's essential to set up separate bank accounts for your business. A good start-up base would include $2,000 to $3,000 in savings, another $2,000 to $3,000 in a checking account with check-writing privileges for approximately 20 checks per month, and a company credit card linked to those accounts. Shop around for the best deal from the banks in your area. Regional banks are usually the best for setting up business accounts as well as applying for loans. They are more likely than larger banks to loan you money and offer the good service that goes with being a "big fish in a small pond." To compare banks, use the above account information, and total the fees and interest that each bank would charge on these services. When you break down the charges for the services you need, it's easy to determine what your best option will be.

Monitoring Expenses and Income

Income, simply stated, is money coming in. Expenses are obviously monies going out. When you balance your expenses against your income, you end up totaling one column and comparing it to the other. This method is very much like balancing a checkbook and is commonly known as the *cash* method of accounting.

The *accrual* method, where expenses are matched to, and directly offset by, the income generated by the jobs on which they are spent, is somewhat impractical for a design studio. Keeping track of art boards or pens and X-Acto knife blades on a per job basis is not feasible. For tax purposes you can choose either the cash or accrual method, but you must stay with that choice for at least six months.

On the freelance or small business level, bookkeeping (keeping tabs on expenditures and income) may be the only accounting you do, so keep good records. In fact, keeping track of what you're taking in and spending is crucial in order to supply records to your accountant, bank and the IRS.

Keeping track of your expenses (debits) and income (credits) is easy with a ledger and disbursement journal. The journal chronologically lists all business exchanges while the ledger categorizes this information according to IRS classifications for

A lot of designers just stumble around with this. Often they are not interested in planning or budgets, but I found the business end of things to be rather creative. I was always somewhat attracted to it. If your goal (at some point) is to run your own show, the best place to learn the ropes is within the arena of another organization, working with smart people and learning from them.

Jilly Simons, Concrete

tax-deductible business expenses. In fact, you can order checkbooks that contain their own ledgers or disbursement sheets. And by organizing your expenses into categories that comply with IRS guidelines, you are also complying with the IRS's requirements for a "contemporaneous log of expenses."

You can go digital with this log — computerize your books! There are a variety of good, small, inexpensive financial programs to use on a Macintosh or IBM-compatible system. In fact, a simple, inexpensive check-writing program may be all you need. I highly recommend computer automation. Hardware prices are dropping and great software is readily available. If this is too high tech or megabuck, you can use the classic Dome Book (a "general ledger") or other "one-write" traditional approaches. Here, checks and journals are aligned sequentially on a peg board with metal guides. Carbons transfer all numbers and information from checks to journals.

Date		Paid By	Amount			Sales (Taxable)	Tax Data Sales Tax (@ 8¼%)	Total Gross Sales
1991								
Jan	16	Caputo Ink	1000.00					
	21	Maxwell	1082.50			1000.00	82.50	
	24	Cooper Co.	541.25			500.00	41.25	
	28	Scarlet Letters	2200.00					
		Totals	4823.75			1500.00	123.75	4700.00

A simple income journal like this one recommended by accountant Juda Kallus is all you really need to keep track of your income and the amount of sales tax you must pay.

Organizing Your Financial Records

In addition to a ledger and journal, you will also need to maintain paper files for keeping track of client invoices, as well as the invoices you receive and pay in the course of doing business. You can keep track of client invoices by setting up three folders, one each for paid, unpaid and partially paid. When you receive full payment, note the date on your invoice and transfer it to the paid file. If you receive partial payment, note the date on your invoice and transfer it to the partially paid folder. When you receive the remaining balance, transfer the invoice to the paid folder.

You will also need to set up an accounts payable file. This would include all project-related invoices you receive as well as your business expenses (phone bills, utilities, rent, etc.). A good method of keeping track is to maintain a file for each day of the month, numbered consecutively. When an invoice comes in on the 20th of a given month, put it in the folder marked 20. On the 20th of the following month, before you insert any new invoices for that day, pull the old invoices that you inserted on the 20th of the last month and pay them that day. This method ensures that you pay all invoices on time, but not until payment is due.

It is also a good idea to maintain the following records. These will supplement the accounting sys-

YOUR NAME
BUSINESS - EXPENSE JOURNAL
JANUARY - FEBRUARY 1989

DATE 1989	PAID TO	CK #	AMOUNT	SUPPLIES	STATS PRINTING TYPOGRAPHY	BOOKS DUES PUBLICAT.	MESSENGERS & DELIVERY	LOCAL TRANSPORT.	MEALS & ENTERTAIN.	TELEPHONE ELECTRICITY	RENT	ADVERTISING	OTHER DESCRIPT.	OTHER AMOUNT
JAN 1	LANDLORD	1	400—								400—			
2	NY TELEPHONE CO.	2	35—							35—				
15	CON EDISON	10	25—							25—				
20	SPEEDY PRINTING CO.	17	275—									275—		
24	ACCURATE TYPESETTING CO.	20	150—		150—									
24	FRIENDLY ART STORE	21	200—	200—										
25	VISA	23	260—	120—		90—		50—					
26	SWIFT MESSENGER CO.	25	26—				26—							
28	ART FURNITURE CO.	28	700—										STUDIO FURNITURE	700—
30	MARVIN THE ACCOUNTANT	30	225—										ACCOUNTING	225—
7	NEIGHBORHOOD HARDWARE STORE	—	15—	15—										
20	STAT HOUSE	—	25—		25—									
25	ART BOOK STORE	—	10—			10—								
31	TRAVEL & MISC. EXPENSE LOG	—	42—			6—	2—	30—		4—				
31	MEALS & ENTERTAINMENT LOG	—	100—						100—					
	TOTALS		2488—	335—	175—	106—	28—	30—	150—	64—	400—	275—		925—
FEB 1	LANDLORD		400—								400—			
2	NY TELEPHONE CO.		32—							32—				
15	CON EDISON		22—							22—				

Keeping track of your expenses is a matter of life or death for your studio. And it's not nearly as hard to do as everyone thinks it is. Maintain your expense journal regularly, as accountant Juda Kallus shows here. Make an entry as you write each check. Divide your expenses into categories that correspond to those on your itemized tax return, and dealing with your obligations to the IRS will be that much easier.

tems mentioned above:
- A cash expense log for meals, travel and entertainment (if there are no receipts or inadequate receipts);
- An appointment and business event diary;
- A travel log for your car to record business-related mileage and tolls;
- If you work at home, devise a method of allocating expenses that are both personal and business (rent or mortgage, utilities, phone and cleaning).

Your IRS Obligations

Be sure to put money away periodically to meet your tax obligations. You are required by law to file quarterly returns with the IRS on April 15, June 15, September 15 and January 15. (These dates may vary by a day or two in any given calendar year.) By the end of the year, 90 percent of what you owe, or 100 percent of what you paid last year is due. Be sure that you comply with the IRS on this. You may have to pay penalties and interest if you do not file or estimate your taxes accurately.

Don't forget that you will also need to pay Self-Employment Social Security tax, based on what you (as your own employer) owe. Your old employer used to make these deductions from your paycheck, but as a self-employed designer you are obligated to pay this tax yourself. This tax is paid annually and

This tax form, which Mary Ann Nichols designed for her husband, Juda Kallus, to use when working with designers, illustrates the different categories of expenses you may deduct.

filed with your regular tax return on April 15.

If you are self-employed, anywhere from 25 to 40 percent of every profit dollar should be set aside for taxes. For further information, make an appointment with your accountant to compute your tax liability based on your projected income. Based on that, he or she will be able to prepare your estimated quarterly taxes.

Plan Now for Retirement

Deferred savings plans make good sense for your future. But profit sharing is too complicated, and pension plans are only appropriate for those with high incomes or large corporations with a great number of employees. But there are alternatives for a small corporation or sole proprietor.

What follows is merely an introduction to some options, not specific tax advice or financial guidelines. A designer should seek an accountant or financial advisor for current information and counseling on ways to minimize taxes and provide for retirement. The best place for your money will vary at any given time, depending on your age and your income at that moment. Needless to say, the economic climate (and forecast) is also subject to change and best managed by those making a living at this sort of thing.

• **IRAs (Individual Retirement Accounts)** currently allow you to save up to $2,000 of your annual income in tax-deferred savings.

• **SEPs (Simplified Employee Pension** plans) allow you to invest more than IRAs permit. Available to any self-employed individual, you can contribute up to 13 percent of your net income. There's a minimum of red tape involved — it's not nearly as complex as defined benefit and contribution plans.

• **Keogh, pension and/or profit-sharing plans** offer greater tax deductions, but involve more paperwork than the above options. Regardless of whether you are a proprietorship, partnership or corporation, you can set up a pension plan or Keogh account for your retirement contributions. There are several different types of plans available exclusively to the self-employed:

Money Purchase Pension Plans (MPPPs) allow you to contribute 20 percent or up to $30,000 a year. When you set up an MPPP, you designate the percentage of your income you'll be putting in each year, and stick to that percentage.

Profit-sharing plans are similar to MPPPs, letting you save up to 13.04 percent or $30,000 annually. The amount you contribute to this plan can vary from year-to-year and might make more sense if your income is not consistent.

• **Defined benefit plans** are based on calculating how much you need to contribute annually in order to receive a specified amount once you retire. With a plan like this you can contribute any amount of your income, even 100 percent, but because they are costly to set up (an actuary needs to make the calculations) these plans are recommended only for those who have high incomes and are close to retirement.

Insurance

First of all, it's crucial to have disability income insurance. If you are laid up, you not only lose your salary, but risk losing your business as well. When determining what kind of coverage you should look into, take into consideration all of your personal obligations, such as mortgages and dependents. Shop for the best coverage rather than the lowest premium, and check for these options when shopping for the best plan:

• A noncancellable policy with guaranteed renewal will forbid the insurer from terminating your policy or increasing your premium after an initial two-year contestability period has passed.

• Policies with a cost-of-living adjustment to keep pace with inflation.

Health care is another expensive but necessary evil. Skimp elsewhere, if you must, but get the best health plan you can afford. Don't make the mistake of thinking you can go even a day without medical coverage. You never know when lightning may strike and, with the exorbitant cost of hospitalization and medical care, you don't ever want to have to pay for medical expenses from your personal funds.

Group Deals
Group insurance rates are frequently lower than those you can obtain as an independent. Many group health care opportunities are available through professional organizations. However, executive organizations or even your local chamber of commerce can frequently offer better rates than the group insurance that is available through design-affiliated professional associations.

Some have speculated that this situation exists because insurance companies view those involved in artistic professions as a high-risk group. Like it or not, professionals in the creative arts (including the visual arts) have been excluded, particularly in recent years, from the kinds of preferential rates available to other professional groups.

An alternative source available in some areas is locally based, self-insured funds for printers and those affiliated with the pre-press end of the graphic arts industry. An independent insurance agent in your area can usually give you the needed information on group opportunities in the graphic arts industry.

Finding the Best Deal for Your Needs
Of course, if you're in good health, you might even find out from your agent that an independent policy will be a better deal than any group benefits. A new business staffed by a young designer should be able to buy life and disability insurance at reasonable rates. Ensure you will obtain the best rates by bypassing obvious risk factors (don't smoke) and preventing peril (install safety equipment).

Consider a number of alternatives when shopping for the best deal. If you feel your only need is to cover yourself in an emergency, you may want to opt for low premium payments on a policy with a high deductible. On the other hand, if you have a family to take care of, a Health Maintenance Organization (HMO) can provide for emergencies as well as offer reduced rates for check-ups and other medical needs.

Should you use different insurance carriers to meet specific needs? This works for many design firms, but if you bundle plans (life insurance, disability and health care) with one carrier, you'll usually get better rates overall. Shop around for the right agent by checking out recommendations and referrals. Once you've found an insurance carrier, diffuse hassles and make sure you are adequately compensated for medical claims by making personal copies of all claim records.

Insurance for Your Business
Investigate these standard areas of coverage when you're starting up:

- **Valuable papers:** Compensates for loss of stolen or damaged artwork and files by covering research time, labor and materials involved. This type of insurance is extremely important when you consider the replacement value of original artwork, transparencies and other films. If you rely on your computer files for maintaining originals, be sure to find out if your coverage in this area includes computer disks as well.
- **Property and liability:** Covers damage to your studio's contents in the event of burglary, robbery, vandalism, or fire and water damage.
- **Liability:** Covers injury to any nonemployee on your premises.
- **Business interruption:** Replaces lost profits if your business is temporarily shut down because of damage to the premises.
- **Auto insurance:** If you're using your car for business and let someone else on your staff drive it, you'll need to add them to your policy.
- **Workers' compensation:** Covers injuries incurred on the job by anyone employed by you (required in most states).
- **Computerized equipment:** Additional coverage beyond general contents in the event of damage by such things as fire or vandalism. Also covers the cost of renting

replacement equipment while your equipment is being repaired.

Finally, if you're working out of your home, you'll want to add a rider on your current homeowner's or renter's insurance to cover damage and theft of your studio property.

Putting Money Back Into Your Studio

Unless you've hit a windfall of profits after operating for a very short period of time, and feel the additional business justifies a loan, you'll need to plan for future growth by regularly investing some of the profits of your business in various accounts. You'll want to invest a portion of it in a liquid account (a passbook savings, or

mainder of your savings into a variety of CD options, money market accounts and mutual funds. The best return on any of these investments will vary at any given time, depending on the current economic situation, so shop around and look for the best alternatives to satisfy your short- and long-range goals. Lock in on the best interest rates available for the savings options that fit your unique needs.

Do You Need Full- or Part-time Help? At start-up, odds are you'll be doing it all. Salaries can take a big bite out of your budget, but at some point you may need to hire a staff.

No doubt, you'll know when the time comes what kind of help you most need, but generally it makes good economic sense to fill an en-

other clerical tasks. You'll want to free yourself to do the work that generates the most income.

Don't hire another full-time designer unless you are sure you can keep that person busy 40 hours per week for a year. It's better to cover a temporary crunch by farming some work out to a freelancer than to hire an employee. You'll not only save the costs of the salary but also the benefits, heavy tax payments, and the furniture and equipment for that person to use.

Loans: If Not Now, Maybe Later

If you have a good credit history and are of sound character, you may have a good chance of getting a loan after having established yourself in business for two to three years. You might even be able to finance a small loan for a piece of equipment after one to two years in business. Start your studio with a good plan for money management and then follow through with it consistently in order to improve your chances of getting a loan. If you keep good financial records from the beginning, you'll easily be able to demonstrate to a skeptical banker why you deserve a loan. Here are 11 steps you can take to become an educated loan applicant when you need additional funds:

1. Be realistic. For a freelancer or small businessperson, the odds of getting a bank loan are just not good. Should you be looking elsewhere for that start-up money?

It's a stair-stepping thing. As you start to grow, you bring in that other designer who thinks the way you do, or hire that much needed business manager. You have to build a foundation, then build on it to create a stronger business.

Joel Fuller, Pinkhaus

money market for instance). Although this type of account won't yield a high interest rate, you'll still be getting some return on monies that are just as accessible to you as the cash in your checking account.

From there, divvy up the re-

try- or intermediate-level position rather than a more qualified one. Consider the following: As studio principal you bill out your time at $60 per hour, but you find yourself spending much of this time answering the phone, filing and doing

2. Go to your accountant for **referrals.** He knows your business, he knows the banks. Get some advice, even ask him to make introductions and open doors for you.

3. Shop around. Visit three separate banks (or more). Evaluate and go with your best deal. A small bank may be the best bet and your local bank is probably your first stop.

4. Lay the groundwork. Build and maintain a loyal relationship (savings and checking accounts) with your bank of choice.

5. Make friends. Build a professional and personal relationship with your banker long before you need a loan.

6. Clean up your house. Reduce your overall debt before you apply for a loan. Establish a solid credit history—repay other loans, and pay them on time.

7. Do your homework. Write a complete business plan. Or at least prepare a loan package (for more on how to prepare a loan package see page 52). Have current fiscal statements (plus past financial summaries) ready for inspection. You'll also need to explain why you need the loan. How much do you need? What kind of loan do you want? Be specific and put it on paper as a proposal. Demonstrate exactly how the money will be used. If you need to make a bona fide presentation with your facts, figures and visuals, do so.

8. Make it easy. Depending on

Is Big Better?

No matter how grandiose your vision or how diminutive your scale, you must maintain high quality in your work—sound advice when you consider that keeping the dollar value of your work up there is the fastest way to get to fat city. High quality work is best achieved through carefully managing the growth of your business. Businesses that make it past the initial hurdles often come to failure because no provisions were made for growth. Grow too fast and you may find yourself in debt and scrambling for work. Fail to anticipate the work load and you might be unable to meet client demands.

There's an old axiom that says, "Be careful what you wish for—you just might get it." Many of the founders of "big" design firms I interviewed waxed romantic about the "good old days" when the company was small—a less hectic calendar; a daily schedule with more breathing room; nominal travel; simpler management styles and procedures; moderate overhead; intimate assignments—the list goes on and on. More than a few yearned to downsize (or had done so already). Our economy taught life lessons to some who were financially forced to retrench or cut back. Several designers spoke from experience when they cautioned that a loss of quality often accompanies rapid growth.

All the designers interviewed started on a modest scale, many working out of their homes. A number of designers remained situated there, in front of the fireplace, because they prefer a more personal business habitat. Others have endeavored to preserve a warm, congenial atmosphere in offices outside the home with loosely constructed, friendly environments designed to foster an open exchange of ideas as well as hard work.

Regardless of the size of their firms, all of the designers interviewed for this book are highly regarded for producing topnotch design and quality service. The size of an operation has little to do with success—it's an individual thing.

your cash flow, you could elect to repay a loan as a single payment. Or pay off a loan in chunks or monthly payments that decrease the principal with remaining interest computed on the unpaid balance. Most loans these days are simple interest loans. Decline a

I'm a little tired after burning the candle at both ends for 20 years. I think about shrinking the firm down (from 15 people) to five people. Once in a while I think about closing. Some days it's terrific and I want to grow more.

Tibor Kalman, M & Co.

loan calculated under the so-called rule of '78s. This strategy is decidedly unfavorable to the borrower, so simply avoid it.

9. Evaluate the rates, study the terms and assess your options. Should you go with a variable rate (which is dictated by the prime lending rate), fixed rate or semi-fixed rate loan?

If you go with a variable rate, is there a ceiling on how high that rate can go (and floor to which it can fall)? If you get a fixed rate, will there be an annual adjustment? Does your lender say, "Mr. Designer, I'll give you a fixed rate, but I'm going to fix it annually at 5 percent over prime"? Make sure that "prime rate" is established by the Treasury Index.

You must be comfortable with the structure of the loan—how and when the debt is repaid and the conditions of payment. What about the term (or duration) of the loan? What you pay on a monthly basis must fit in with your cash flow. A four-year loan lowers your monthly payment, but ultimately will cost you more in interest. Can you pay off the loan early, or will you be hit with prepayment penalties? Understand your loan agreement completely. Don't look just at the dollar cost of the loan—it really comes down to getting the best rate and terms you can get (and live with).

10. Turn down the extras. You don't need the bank's credit, life or disability insurance. These options (they're not mandatory) only jack up the end costs of the loan.

11. Go for it. Yes, it's true that little percentage points can add up to big bucks, but you can't predict if (or when) interest rates will go up or down. You could lose your best opportunity by waiting until rates are at their lowest point.

You'll need to prepare a loan package before making your presentation to the bank. This important formal document should cover the last three years (remember the current quarter, too) and include:

- Company history (keep it to just one page);
- Principals' résumés (again, one page per individual);
- Statement about the use of the loan (a simple but specific list of categories and amounts is fine);
- Profit and loss statement, including balance sheets and a record of current accounts receivable and payable;
- Cash flow statement;
- Three-year cash flow projection;
- Statement of your terms, pricing and company policies;
- Personal and business tax returns (ask how many years);
- Equipment index or inventory list;
- Customer and supplier references (three to five for each);
- Personal guaranty.

Unfortunately, most lenders will insist you personally guarantee a loan. Neither the tight relationship you've established with your banker nor the heavyweight business you've set up will spare you this considerable risk. If you need the money, you'll just have to bite the bullet. You might just look at a personal guaranty as yet another means of showing the bank that you are a good risk.

When applying for a loan a comprehensive business plan will also be a big plus. (See pages 49-52 for a detailed discussion on business plans.)

Systems Evolve for Better Management

Read Viemeister is astonished when asked about how his studio, Vie Design, in Yellow Springs, Ohio, became so successful. "I'm surprised that it's worked as well as it has," he responds. "After all, being in one location for 40 years — a tiny town of 4,000 people — is sort of weird."

Because Viemeister's background is in both industrial and graphic design, Vie Design is a home for both disciplines. Its current staff of five has done industrial design for a wide range of products, including bikes, power mowers and electric ranges. It also produces sales catalogs, annual reports, corporate identity and other printed materials.

Vie Design started very modestly. Viemeister uprooted himself from a secure design position in New York City in order to be closer to his wife (at that time his fiancé), who was finishing her education at Antioch University in Yellow Springs. "I began at Lippincott & Doner right after graduating from Pratt Institute," says Viemeister. He spent four years at the firm that later became Lippincott & Margulies. "I left a very, very good job in New York — my parents thought I was out of my mind to quit my job and get married.

"I realized I had to do something to earn a living," says Viemeister, recalling some of the scrambling he did for needed income. "I did a lot of work for the college — cartoons and illustration." Viemeister was fortunate to land a part-time job heading the industrial design department at the Dayton Art Institute, which supplied him with steady income while he continued to generate business in the Yellow Springs community.

With his background in industrial design, Viemeister soon found he was able to capitalize on the area's industrial-based economy and the boom in advertising that developed in the post-war economy. "This was right after World War II," he says. "I was working with an agency concentrating on industrial advertising. There was a lot of excitement there — I was able to inject a lot of design thinking into their industrial advertising."

Viemeister's business continued to grow, prompting him to take on a partner. "I contacted a former classmate, Bud Steinhilber, who joined me about '49," he says. "From about 1955 to 1965 we built many client bases, and the two of us performed very well together as a team. This proved beneficial to our gradual and steady growth. After the war we grew along with everybody else — industry, advertising and design."

The firm's recordkeeping systems have evolved over decades of growth, but started as a humble 3-by-5-inch box filled with index cards (one for each client or job). "The switch from those index cards to our current three-piece tracking system was generated because our volume increased," Viemeister remembers. "We needed a better system of control.

"We established a system in the '50s," says Viemeister, "that involves three cards for each project." One copy of these job cards (the master) goes to the accounting department to keep track of all job-related time and expenses, which are coded by job number. Two columns are maintained and totaled on each card. One column records the actual dollar and time amount for various tasks and purchases (with purchases marked up the standard 20 percent). The other column indicates the amount quoted to the client. When the job is completed, the time and expenses on all three cards are totaled for the final bill. This system enables Viemeister to track and compare expenses as well as measure his profit (or loss) margin on a per-job basis.

While the master copy of the job card remains in accounting, the two remaining copies travel through production with the project so costs may be recorded immediately. "The second copy of the card is stapled onto a large envelope. This envelope is the proj-

ect's job jacket. This card is ultimately removed from the job jacket and sent to accounting when all work is finished," Viemeister says. "The third copy is with the designer responsible for the job. Because he works on several assignments during the day, this designer records the job number (plus activities and time spent) on his daily time sheet. That time sheet goes back to our accounting people and they transfer the time onto the master card for their records."

Thus, all job-related purchases and information (item, purchase order date and place of purchase) are recorded on the accounting department's master job card. "As long as every job in the shop has a number, costs and hours for that job can be readily identified," Viemeister states.

Viemeister does his invoicing on a monthly basis. "Client billing is done on computer, as well as our monthly statements and business analysis," he tells us. At billing time, he goes through his master job cards and organizes them by stages (where each job may be at that point in time). "We don't wait until a job is completed and delivered to invoice the client," he points out. "If a job has been designed, the creative work is done and the job is in production. That's when we bill for our creative time. After production and delivery, we'll invoice again.

"Knowing what's happening (from a dollar standpoint) at any time, keeping close tabs on your costs, is essential. It's really the most important part of operating a business, whether it's a one-man shop, or a ten-person operation."

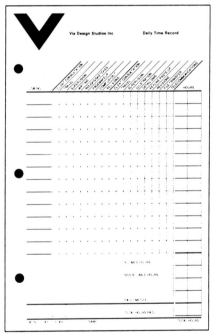

These daily time cards are an integral part of Vie Design's efficient record-keeping system. The designer records the job number plus activities and time spent and sends the card to the accounting people. They then transfer the time records to the master card for each job.

Over the years Vie Design has produced a broad range of projects for its diverse clients, such as the handcrafted wall hanging shown here.

The Domino Effect

As a high school co-op in 1976, Theo Stephan ran a stat camera for a Dayton, Ohio, department store. It was an excellent apprenticeship, however, and Stephan stayed with the store through college, until 1982. "I worked my way up in the advertising department," she remembers. "I literally did everything—layout design, conceptual stuff, finished pieces. I worked with the copywriter and went to photo shoots in New York."

Stephan moved on in 1983. As production manager in another retail position, she learned how to work with advertising agencies. Here she discovered "media—radio and television—the actual advertising end of the industry."

Her business happened "by mistake," she says with a smile. "I quit my job and started to freelance with agencies. Everybody told me that my portfolio was too retail-

oriented. So I freelanced for two years to get more of those agency-type pieces in my book. But my goal was not to start my own business; it was to work as an art director in an agency."

However, business "became overwhelming." In 1985, Stephan's studio, Real Art, was born when Stephan made the jump from

her bedroom studio to a separate office and hired another designer. One year later an increase in business necessitated hiring a production person. An office manager was brought in just one year later as sales continued to grow. Her business continues to thrive and Real Art is now six strong (an accountant, sales rep and four artists). Future plans for growth call for sales offices in Indianapolis, Indiana, *and* Columbus, Ohio, too.

"I found myself being pulled away from what I really wanted—and needed—to do," Stephan recalls. "It's hard to justify growth and adding staff when you know you can 'simply do it yourself,' when you know it 'only means a couple of extra hours after work.' So, then a 50 hour week turns into a 60 hour week, and you end up doing all these things that you really don't do best anyway . . . you just get burned out.

"It's the domino effect. Growth creates capabilities, which in turn makes you busier, which in turn means you need more people."

This 1988 Christmas card promotes Real Art Design in a fun way. It also documents the studio's growth. Her 1986 card mentioned only Theo Stephan; the 1988 card is from Real Art "angels" Betsy, Colleen, Melissa and Theo.

Mary Ann Nichols

The Electronic Manager

With 10 years as a graphic designer under her belt, Mary Ann Nichols decided to set up her own studio, Nichols Graphic Design, in 1978. Her experience, business contacts, and the support of friends and colleagues made the New York City designer confident she could manage her own business.

"In the beginning," Nichols admits, "I didn't have that many projects, so it wasn't so difficult to keep track of them. But as I got busier, I became more organized and created a sheet for price quotes. This recorded when a call came in, the price I quoted and some basic info. I kept the sheet in a loose-leaf notebook, so I could refer to it when that contact came back to me.

"I had learned to use job jackets and store everything in a convenient location, so, over the years I was producing and storing graphic design in the traditional way. The last four years I've switched over to the computer. Most of, if not all of, my work is now generated on the Macintosh. A lot of what I do is

filed electronically. I still have job files but don't need that much room for the big envelopes any more. Most of the time, I have my clients take care of color separations and printing so the printer holds that material."

Thanks to her husband, an accountant, Nichols uses customized software to monitor expenses and income. She strongly advocates utilizing the computer to simplify what is, for many, a daunting task.

"I don't have that many out-of-pocket cash expenses. I make a loose-leaf folder and I generate a form for each month. Then I just list what the expense is, the date, and what it was for. There's a folder behind this where I stick in the receipt. I input this info when I do my monthly books.

"You *can* do your books . . .

even if you don't have a mate who's an accountant," she says with a grin. "I definitely recommend that designers get a computer and find some small business software. People should be doing their accounts monthly (it also helps with quarterly taxes). Don't wait until the last minute, at the end of the year, to figure out how you're doing. . . . The computer makes it all so simple. It's certainly made my life easier — I have far more time to do my design business and spend less time on my accounting."

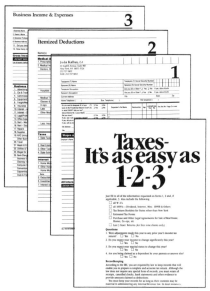

Nichols designed this series of easily comprehensible tax forms for her husband, Juda Kallus, an accountant whose specialty is tax preparation for artists and designers. The cover sheet clearly and concisely ensures that Kallus's clients supply all necessary paperwork to their accountant. Heading the forms with large, bold numbers further simplifies matters.

nichols

Mary Ann Nichols
Graphic Designer
80 Eighth Avenue
Suite 900
New York, NY 10011-5126

212 727-9818
212 727-9812 FAX

Nichols's business card is simple but still quite effective. It's also relatively inexpensive since it's one-color printing on colored stock.

CHAPTER 7

BRINGING IN CLIENTS

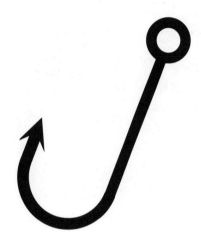

We've talked in earlier chapters about why designers are not as business-minded as they should be. Likewise, many designers are not good salespeople either. Perhaps the problem is really one of attitude rather than a lack of ability. Maybe designers fear the image of some high-pressure huckster peddling substandard, unwanted goods. Maybe they hold the mistaken notion that any sales activity is below their creative station.

In truth, sales are the lifeblood of your business, so how do we get past these counterproductive notions? It might help to develop this mindset: You are calling on clients to see if you can help. So think "How can I help you?" instead of "Do you want to buy?" As designer Ellen Shapiro points out, "As soon as I can, I change the meeting from me selling work to me helping them with their communication problem."

You need to sell. If you're convinced that by doing so you're reduced to pushing snake oil, your business will go nowhere. It's crucial that you believe in what you are doing. And what you are doing is solving problems—a most valuable service and worthwhile endeavor. If you must sell something to make a living, creative solutions make for a wonderful product. Don't you agree? Within this chapter you'll learn more about how to sell this potent elixir, where to find clients, and how to make effec-

tive—no, truly *dynamic*—presentations. You'll find out how to keep clients hungry for more so you won't have to go out on a sales hunt with every new job. Let's get busy!

Step 1: Find Clients

Finding clients who need your services is a bit like running a dating service. You're matchmaking your special abilities to the folks who have the greatest need for them. This sounds simple, but figuring out where to focus your energies involves some thought and planning. It might be best to first break your possibilities down into several business groups in order to isolate where potential business may be:

• **Business/private enterprise:** The possibilities are endless. Is the real estate market booming in your area? Think of ways your skills could be used in creating promotions for real estate agents trying to sell property. Do you have a flair for restaurant identities and menu design? Now you get the picture—think about where your skills can best be applied.

• **Ad agencies/design studios:** When you're on your own you're in a good position to handle the overflow coming from any and all aspects of the business. Possibilities beyond traditional design and mechanical production include calligraphy or typographic design, illustration and storyboarding, art

directing photo shoots, and more.

• **Publishers:** Every town has a newspaper, and most cities have at least one publisher of books and magazines. Again, you're in a good position to handle any of the overflow. Find out when the most demanding times are for the publications in your area. (Is there a magazine in your area that publishes a special issue, demanding more work from its in-house art staff for a short period of time?) Contact them when you think the production for that peak period is in the planning stages.

• **Graphic arts supplier:** This classification includes color houses, print shops and service bureaus. Printers, in particular, frequently seem to find themselves in need of production skills when a client "dumps" a job on them that was supposedly camera-ready. Even if a printer has his own typesetting and production services, clients will frequently need more design skills than a production staff can supply.

In addition to thinking about where you can market your work, also think about your proficiency level and match your skills to prospective clients accordingly. If you're just starting out in your career, you'll want to go to quick-print and small shops, rather than your city's largest and most reputable four-color printer. Until you've gained some experience and credibility, your design skills may be better suited to smaller businesses than that multimillion dollar corporation downtown.

Also consider your design style, and how it matches up with the image a prospective client presents. Does the work in your portfolio reveal an eye for the trendy design that interests a new boutique owner, or is your design lean and conservative — more appropriate for a law firm or doctor's office?

her business if you cleaned up her image by designing a new card?

Remember, you're not selling a service so much as you're solving communication problems. The professionals you know or do business with all want to improve their visibility and profitability. Look for situations where your work can make a difference. You may already have the inside line on business possibilities through a former employer. Any situation where you

local professional groups can provide great opportunities to find some of the most lucrative markets in your area. Possibilities include your local art directors club or AIGA. When you attend meetings, find out who other designers are working for. Are they swamped? Let them know you're looking for any business they can't handle or any job with which they don't want to get involved.

Don't overlook professional groups affiliated with the communications field or other executive organizations. These people are often looking for support services they can use in their work and frequently are in need of design skills. Possibilities include local groups for editors, public relations specialists and ad clubs. Groups like these frequently publish and distribute directories for members and other business professionals as a source of services in the community.

Small-budget clients are a lot more flexible . . . more naive about design. They don't know exactly what they want, so they'll give you more freedom to explore possibilities. I think when you get into the big projects, it comes down to fear on the part of the client. They think, "I'm spending $700,000 on this annual report — I'd better not take a chance."

Tibor Kalman, M & Co.

Leads

Look for potential business wherever you go. Does your oral surgeon have a hard time explaining surgical procedures to you? Could he use a brochure that explains these procedures? It's getting close to tax time and your accountant jots her number down on scrap paper because she ran out of business cards. If she's too busy to take care of getting them printed, could you do it for her? Could she increase

once worked is bound to yield potential. Don't forget, you're already familiar with the work and the work habits of these people, and they see this familiarity as a plus.

Networking

Beyond looking for business potential within your sphere of influence, you should seek specific opportunities for networking that will yield referrals and leads. In addition to providing a good support system,

Step 2: Promote Yourself

Self-promotion can take many forms. You can advertise, list your services in directories, and contact prospective clients by phone or by mail. As a graphic designer you are most likely promoting print capability more than anything else. We're not ignoring visual presentations, displays and environmental design, but most graphic design business consists of print commu-

Ruby Shoes Studio's "Fan Club Card" is a Rolodex card that makes it easy for potential clients not only to remember the studio's name but also to find the address and phone number when a job comes up.

nication. So it makes sense to consider promoting yourself with printed materials as your first order of business.

The Self-Promotion Piece

The self-promotional mailer is a vehicle many designers depend upon to showcase their work. When the primary purpose of a self-promotional mailer is to dazzle and entice its recipient, creative license knows no boundaries. We've seen bottles of wine and beer with custom labels, fortune cookies with messages enclosed, even hula hoops that have been sent to prospective clients as part of a direct mail campaign.

More traditional concepts like posters and calendars — if they're really good or useful — may be displayed on a client's wall, perhaps doubling your promo's visibility. Clever mailers are frequently passed along. ("Look what I got in the mail today. I know you'll appreciate this.") This expands their

impact beyond the initial recipient.

If you're looking for inspiration, scope out the glut of annuals and creative directories available. Within these admired pages you'll view today's most creative and beautifully designed self-promo

If they're attractively designed and effectively showcase your work, black-and-white promotional pieces such as these for Art Direction Inc. give you more promotion for less money. You should always target your pieces carefully — someone who needs small, low-budget ads could be turned off by a cutting edge or heavily designed piece.

pieces. *CA* and *Print* magazines (and most local competitions) include a category for self-promotion. *HOW* magazine has devoted an entire competition to self-promotion, featuring the winners in an annual special issue.

There are almost as many occasions — or excuses, depending on how you look at them — for mailing out self-promotional pieces as there are types of self-promotional vehicles. Seasonal (not necessarily just holiday) greetings, a change of address, acquiring a partner — all these qualify as opportunities for you to showcase your best work in a self-promotional piece.

Since this book is about starting up a studio, we'll concentrate on the importance of direct mail self-promotion as a means of letting people know you're in business and that you're looking for clients. You want to intrigue a prospective client with a promo piece that demonstrates the high caliber of your work, so you'll want it to be one of the best designed and best crafted things you've ever done.

Capabilities Brochures

A generic self-promotional vehicle, known as the capabilities brochure, is frequently used by designers for its versatility. A capabilities brochure often provides a glimpse of a designer's portfolio by providing a photographic representation of some of their best work. Don't be limited by the concept of a traditional bound-with-a-cover brochure. It can be a single, folded 11-by-17-inch sheet, as well as any other size, shape or format. However, capabilities brochures do have some standard information in common:

•**Client information:** You'll want to provide a list of the firms you've worked with, making sure to include the ones that have the most prestige and are most recognized. If you're just starting out, providing a client list may be difficult to do, but if you were a staff designer before going out on your own you have a right to claim the design and production work for which you were responsible. Check first with your former employer to find out if they would be opposed to your listing a few of their clients with whom you have worked.

•**Background:** Think of this as your résumé. You'll want to include information about your education and your awards. Include any experience or achievements that will enhance your credibility as a creative professional.

•**Capabilities:** You want to spell out everything you can do and leave no stone unturned. Whether it be handling a major identity program, outdoor advertising, magazine illustration—if you can do it, name it. If you have typesetting facilities on the premises, access to top-notch copywriting, or do your own photography, mention it. This is where you mention all of your studio's capabilities.

•**Your design philosophy:** This is where you do your best to convince prospective clients that your work can be more beneficial to them than any other designer's work.

•**Contact information:** Don't forget your address and phone number!

Balancing creative expression with the information prospective clients need about your business is where experience (or lack of it) comes into play. If you have worked with many high-profile clients, you'll want to play this up for credibility. But, if you're just starting out, you'll want to demonstrate potential. Your self-promotional piece is the best vehicle you have to show what you can do. In essence it says, "I got you to notice this direct mail piece and consider hiring me. I could help you be noticed by your prospective clients." Trust your gut on balancing the need to demonstrate your creative abilities with the need to communicate your credibility in a clear and concise way.

Direct Mail

We've talked about the capabilities brochure as a vehicle for introducing your firm to prospective clients. The brochure tells anyone and everyone what you and your firm can do. But does it tell Mr. Spacely how you're going to help him sell more sprockets? Does it point out specific benefits to any of your prospective clients? This is where a cover letter, tailored to your prospect, personalizes your mailing and lets you spell out benefits specific to the prospect's needs. For instance, if you want to get a firm's logo and identity business, you'll want to tell the person responsible for making this decision why you're most qualified to do this. Include information about working up an identity for XYZ Corporation, and the logo you developed for a local magazine. Include a separate sheet within your capabilities brochure that consists of nothing but printed logo samples. If you've

This three-panel, self-mailing promo piece for Art Direction Inc. includes a business reply card for a potential client's response. The card invites the recipient to contact Art Direction about a job, to request a portfolio review, or to receive future mailings. Whatever the response, Art Direction will file this contact name, title and phone number for future promotion and marketing efforts.

done some homework on what this company needs, mention specifically what you can do to fill the gap.

If you want to pitch to a market segment, promoting your work to several firms with similar needs, use a generic cover letter and personalize it with the individual's name, company and address. Be sure to address your contact by name in the salutation of your letter. Do a mailing to prospective clients, multiplying the effectiveness of your letter by addressing concerns common to that particular segment of the market.

Mailing Lists

Let's take the example of the logo letter that you composed above. If you obtain a list of new businesses from your local Chamber of Commerce, you'll have a list of prospective clients to whom you can mail your cover letter and a capabilities brochure. Your mailing list needs will depend on the nature of your skills and who you think will buy your services. You can consult the Yellow Pages and research directories at your local library and bookstore for leads. Browse creative directories and scan client lists. Special interest publications will often sell their lists, making them available through a broker (who can turn you on to even more list possibilities).

If you own a computer, database software is useful for maintaining and organizing lists. Besides making use of this data in your mailings, you can also use this software to figure out from where you're getting your best response.

Talent Directories

There are several national talent directories that list designers, illustrators and photographers by service and by geography. Major metropolitan regions have talent directories as well. Art directors (especially in agencies and periodical publishing) will browse through these books studying the photographers' and illustrators' full-page ads. It's very easy for an art director to spot a look he or she likes, and then phone to order the style of their choice.

These types of directories may not be as advantageous an avenue for graphic designers as for illustrators, particularly for start-ups, unless you have a specialty that someone is likely to buy as a support service, such as typographic design, illustration or calligraphy. If you're networking with other designers in your area you're probably aware of whether or not a local directory is available in your region, and if there is one, how useful it is to designers in your community. Again, the insights of other designers are your inside line to the best opportunities in your area.

Phone Directories

The most overlooked opportunity for visibility may be your local Yellow Pages. Don't take this avenue for granted—you'll have to have a business line installed in order to qualify. If you're doing business out of your home on a residential line, Ma Bell won't give you an opportunity to be listed or buy an ad.

A listing in your city's business-to-business directory could also be a good opportunity for improving your accessibility, and one that will give you increased credibility as a bona fide business. Again, you will have to have a business line installed in order to qualify. (By the way, these always cost more than residential service.)

Finally, don't overlook directories such as the Yellow Pages or business-to-business phone directory as a source of categorized business listings for making cold calls.

Television and Radio Advertising

You may want to consider local media advertising as another marketing and promotional tool. Radio to sell graphic design? Sure — a sharp, creative radio spot fuels the visuals of the imagination. If done well, your message will definitely get across.

Television time will be pricey, but a good 15- or 30-second spot may be money extremely well spent. You might consider an announcement on your cable channel's community calendar or a late, late night television spot (when ad rates are dirt cheap).

Cold Calls

A cold call — person-to-person, by letter or phone — is a contact without request and often without referral. It's essentially selling door-to-door, and as such can be pure frustration. It's a certified way to test your tolerance for rejection, but a persuasive salesman can get a good return for his troubles.

To build a list of contacts, consult the Yellow Pages. Go to the library or bookstore to research directories and look through publications. Browse the creative directories and scan client lists. At-

tend trade shows (and read trade publications). Send for annual reports. Join your local ad club. Visit the Better Business Bureau and Chamber of Commerce. Take a stroll through the business district. Talk to your friends and colleagues.

When making calls to potential clients, use proper phone etiquette. Identify yourself to your prospect or the person who fields their calls. If you can't get through, leave a detailed, but concise, message stating who you are, what you do, and how you think you can help this individual. If you make contact with your prospect, go through the same identifying process, then clear this person's time by asking, "Do you have a minute to talk?" If he says he is tied up, ask for a specific time when you can call back, and return the call promptly at that time. By doing this, you'll be demonstrating courtesy and prompt follow-up skills.

So you landed that first meeting? Great! You've done your research, right? You have found out all you can about this prospect before the scheduled appointment. You're completely prepared.

Face-to-face, blend the business discussion into a friendly conversation. No hard sell — try a soft approach and avoid the sales pitch. Simply chat to learn more about the prospect and the project. You're just seeking an exchange of information at this point. Show your portfolio. Use an initial get-

Mike Salisbury ran this dynamic promotional piece in *Adweek Portfolio* to show the breadth of the agency's work.

Ten Steps to Telemarketing Success

You should view cold calls as just another avenue for pursuing yet more business. Getting in the door to see your prospect is the initial hurdle, so getting on the horn is your first step.

Working the phones (telemarketing) won't be a walk down easy street, but can ultimately lead to a path paved with gold (not to mention clichés).

1. First, do your research. Find out all you can about a potential client before you attempt to schedule an appointment. Be completely prepared.
2. Are you calling the right person? Consult the directories or, if necessary, make a preliminary call to the company switchboard.
3. When you land a meeting, get an exact address and good directions before you get off the phone.
4. Calling back for any of the above information makes you look unprofessional, so get it right the first time.
5. Establish a balance of great confidence, reasonable goals and realistic expectations. This chemistry will keep you from getting discouraged too fast and quitting too soon.
6. Have patience, perseverance and a positive attitude.
7. Remember, you are not selling anything with a first phone call. No pressure now, so relax. You just want to get together.
8. Have all of your information in front of you (a calendar, appointment book, client information, a list of clients and references).
9. If the ball is in your court, suggest a meeting date with alternatives. Be flexible enough to rearrange your schedule if necessary.
10. Every call will present a new challenge, so pay attention to both negative reactions and positive replies. Note your responses to all of these scenarios. Study (and practice) what does and doesn't work as your telemarketing campaign continues.

Don't get easily discouraged. Learn from your rejections, and your calls will succeed—the appointments will come in. And, since you'll be spending lots of time on the phone, you'll have plenty of opportunities to develop your communication skills. Now get out there and make that sale!

together to present design solutions that suggest how you can solve the client's communication problems. Observe closely and keep your ears open. Talk less, listen more. At this point you're just trying to determine if the potential for doing business exists.

Genially probe for information with phrases such as, "I'm curious about. . . . I'd like to know. . . . Please elaborate on this. . . ." Schmooze a bit with flattery: "Tell me more about your great work at Amalgamated Anagrams. What's it like to be employed with such a hot company?"

If there is a definite assignment up for grabs, you could say, "I'd like to hear more about your wonderful product and what the firm has done in the past. Can you tell me about this exciting project? Why are you taking this new direction? What are your goals?"

Once fact finding is over, you will eventually have to inquire about money. Simple, direct inquiries work well: "What's your budget on something like this?" or "How much do you want to spend here?"

The client might volley the ball back to your court and inquire what you would charge for such an assignment. Your reply might be, "All clients are not the same. Every job is different. For projects similar to this, I've charged $XXX; this is based on . . . (detail your pricing structure and related particulars)."

By the way, certain advisors tell you to give a range between X and Z, while others warn you to never ball-park—always state a firm figure. You'll have to decide what feels and works best for you.

Of course, you will ultimately ask for the prospect's business at some point. Make it easy for both parties with phrases that suggest this possibility such as, "Great, what if we . . . ? So where do we go from here? Does this sound do-able? Let me run this by you. . . . Shall we . . . ?"

Competitions

The best credibility in the world, and a testament to your capabilities as a designer, are design competitions. Design competitions are almost always judged by designers who have gained recognition for their own design capabilities and won many competitions themselves. In addition to recognition from your peers, competition awards attest to the top quality of your work and ultimately justify a high level of compensation for your talent and ability. These awards also look great on the wall of your reception area. They are your "credentials"—easily recognizable as such to anyone who walks into your office and has not yet been exposed to the wonderful samples of your work you are about to show them.

There are competitions sponsored by national magazines—*CA*

> We have someone who makes the first call to clients, but we don't have a salesperson. Salespeople always misrepresent your position. I also don't want to take every project. A salesperson feels that their responsibility is to get you every job. You end up with a lot of work you don't want, things that are misrepresented, and with an unnecessary layer between you and your clients.
>
> *Tibor Kalman, M & Co.*

Any event in your life or your studio's life represents an opportunity for great self-promotion. Theo Stephan used this clever flip book inspired by *The Wizard of Oz* (above) to announce her studio's 1988 change of address. When Real Art Design Group, Inc., moved again just two years later, Stephan chose this "Moving Violation" concept (right) for her announcement. The invitation to the open house resembled a subpoena—having some fun with so much moving.

> **First qualify the prospect. Make sure that every meeting is worthwhile, that the client is actually looking for a designer. Make sure that there is indeed something the prospect needs (and a job for which you'll be considered). You don't want to do a meeting just for the sake of meeting. However, when you're just starting, you may have no choice.**
>
> *Ellen Shapiro, Shapiro Design Associates*

and *Print* are the best known for this and publish annuals that are highly revered for showcasing the best in the United States. Other prestigious national competitions include the CLIO Awards, the Society of Publication Designers National Awards, and the New York Art Directors Club's annual competition.

You'll also find a wealth of local opportunities through professional organizations (the local Addy's, your Art Directors Club, Editors Association, etc.). You're probably already aware of many of them — you know which ones offer the most prestige in your area.

If you enter a competition and find you have a winner, get some mileage out of this piece by entering it in another competition. If it walked away with a gold award at your local art directors club competition, send it off to a national competition. And don't forget public-

ity. When you win an award, let your clients know about it — especially the client for whom you did the award-winning work. You'll want to notify them personally if this piece has won some recognition. They may want to promote the award themselves within their company and your community, giving you additional exposure.

The best way to "toot your own horn" in a professional manner is to send out a press release to your other clients, local news media, na-

tional design magazines and trade publications (if you feel the prestige of this award is worthy of national recognition).

If you've produced work for a client whose trade has its own competition for design excellence, you'll also want to know if he or she has plans to enter anything you've done for them in their industry's competition. Let this individual know that you value the quality of the work you did for them and would appreciate notification of any awards within their industry that the printed piece may garner.

Pro Bono Work

Donating your design services can be an excellent means of receiving publicity. The trade-off you make with the group commissioning the work is your skill in exchange for a credit on the printed piece. You usually have the chance to do your own thing, thus you gain an opportunity to showcase your talents. Local arts and theater groups will

> **Being articulate is extremely important. You need to be able to walk into a boardroom full of decision makers who don't know beans about graphic design and be able to explain the job on a level that gets them excited and gains their trust.**
>
> *Rex Peteet, Sibley/Peteet Design*

Competitions to Consider

Contact these competitions for information on deadlines and entry fees:

Competition	Sponsor	Contact
Addys	American Advertising Federation	1400 K St., Ste. 1000 Washington, DC 20005 (800) 828-8225
Annual of American Illustration	Society of Illustrators	128 E. 63rd St. New York, NY 10010 (212) 838-2560
Art Directors Annual	New York Art Directors Club	250 Park Ave. New York, NY 10003 (212) 674-0500
CA Design Annual	*Communication Arts* magazine	410 Sherman Ave. Box 10300 Palo Alto, CA 94303 (415) 326-6040
HOW Self-Promotion Competition	*HOW* magazine	1507 Dana Ave. Cincinnati, OH 45207 (513) 531-2222
Print's Regional Design Annual	*Print* magazine	104 Fifth Ave. New York, NY 10011 (212) 463-0600

frequently offer a talented designer opportunities for high exposure through posters and other promotional vehicles. There's nothing like seeing your work all over town.

Other possibilities for pro bono work include charity fundraisers (walkathons, road races and charity balls). The people who run these events and volunteer their services are often the movers and shakers in your community. They're frequently in a good position to circulate your name. And they may be sources of future business.

Another advantage to pro bono work is the caliber of the support services at your disposal. Frequently top-quality printers and service bureaus will donate their services for a charitable event, allowing you to familiarize them with your capabilities. You'll also have a chance to use services and goods that budget-conscious clients may not have afforded you.

And don't forget you may donate your time to the firms offering support services in exchange for a collaboration on a promotional piece. Printers and color houses also are often looking for good design vehicles to demonstrate their capabilities.

Your Portfolio

Your portfolio speaks volumes for your abilities as a graphic designer. If you're unable to present your portfolio personally, it should offer as descriptive and as effective a presentation as you would offer if you were there to explain the work yourself.

Be selective about what you include in your portfolio. Young designers tend to show their best work, but dilute it with anything they have that's been printed. A dozen of your most representative pieces often are sufficient. Organize the presentation so the best and most eye-catching pieces are the first ones viewed.

Art directors and others who spend a lot of time looking at portfolios say that the portfolio should be viewed as a design project in itself. Your portfolio demonstrates presentation capabilities, packaging design, and intelligent strategy to market a most important concept—you, the *designer*. Your portfolio should be neat and well-crafted. A sloppy appearance, or one that is not unified, will give the impression of a designer who cares little about craftsmanship. If your portfolio is not well organized, it will convey the impression of a designer who doesn't think logically. Experts in portfolio design say that the best way to unify a presentation is to make everything consistent. If you have transparencies or printed pieces in several different sizes, mat

Six Tips for a Good Presentation

New York designer Mary Ann Nichols offers these pointers to make a client meeting more productive (and profitable):

1. *Do some research.* Who are you seeing? What do they do? Who are their clients? What do they need? Can you provide a service they need? If so, tell them how you can benefit them.

2. *Look presentable and be courteous.* You have only one chance to make a good first impression—use it. Always shake hands, make eye contact, introduce yourself and be polite.

3. *Be confident and listen carefully.* Point out your strengths, have a positive attitude, and suggest how your skills can benefit the client. Listen attentively for advice and suggestions.

4. *Organize your portfolio.* Keep like assignments together—logos with logos, posters with posters, packaging with pack-

aging. If you have designed a logo and are showing applications of it, keep them together. Don't be redundant—it's not necessary to show the same design in 20 different color combinations.

5. *Never apologize for your work.* If you are dissatisfied with a piece in your book, take it out or redo it. Never show anything that is not your best. A few excellent pieces are far better to show than many mediocre ones. After all, your goal is to leave a good impression.

6. *Thank the interviewer and leave your calling card.* Always thank the person you have seen for his or her time and help. Remember to leave behind a copy of your capabilities brochure and a business card or your résumé and a printed sample of your work. This helps the interviewer remember you and your work.

them consistently so the color and exterior dimensions are the same. Subtle touches like embossed leather give an added touch of quality and often convey the image that you are a success and can afford the best. It might be wise to make this investment, rather than pinching pennies on a cheap vinyl portfolio

if you're trying to impress high-profile clients.

If you must mail portfolio materials to a prospective client, stack matted print pieces in a custom-made container that fits within a shipping container. This will make for a much neater presentation than pulling some samples out of

your portfolio case and dumping them into an envelope.

While designing your portfolio, you may want to consider putting together interchangeable components so your portfolio can be tailored to a variety of situations. For example, if you're trying to sell your services as a book jacket designer, you would want to include more samples of the work you've done in this area than samples of brochures and annual reports.

Read Viemeister of Vie Design says that the pieces included should "demonstrate your sketching ability, your rendering talent," as well as design capabilities. He points out that a graphic designer should "show sketch layouts for proposals, maybe a comprehensive layout with the finished printed piece. This way, a client can see how capably a designer can present concepts before they are committed to print." Viemeister also makes a case for explaining how you solved the problem at hand in every project you present. "Be clear about what your responsibilities were—if you handled the overall organization, say so. A lot of customers are not familiar with the design process at all, and they'll want to know the specifics. 'Here's a rough layout of what we did on the XYZ project. Here's the comp, and here's the finished piece.' The client will see this stage and get the impression that you know what you're doing every step of the way."

Viemeister offers these final words of caution. "Bits and pieces in a loose-leaf book, wrinkled and folded, don't make it," he comments. "A client will say, 'If you don't value your own work, how are you going to value the work you might do for me?'"

Step 3: Keep the Clients You Get

Service—being reliable, on time, returning phone calls promptly, following up, and personally (and personably) ramrodding the job—is the name of the game. Call it every cliché in the book: going the extra mile, hand-holding, TLC, doing whatever it takes. Cozy, and oft-used, these homilies are nevertheless (if I dare use one more) right on the money.

Some things you probably already know or suspect about dealing with clients include: 1) That a prima donna with an I-don't-care-about-you attitude, no matter how good he or she may be, will only generate and keep business for so long. 2) Unless they're masochists, people don't honestly want to work with someone who doesn't care about or won't take care of them. Would you? 3) Given a choice, a client will prefer the designer known for good work and personal service over the hot, creative Garbo wannabe ("I vant to design alone").

Consider the amount of time you've spent in acquiring business—how promoting yourself and cultivating new accounts eats into your billable time. Getting and keeping clients who keep coming back will free you up to bill out more of your time. Clients who keep coming back because you reliably take good care of them are also more likely to do everyone a good turn by passing your name on to those with whom they do business.

The "Big" Accounts

It is entirely possible to keep your studio going with small to medium accounts. Obviously, your volume of business will have to rise accordingly. However, "big" is relative. Your bread-and-butter account may be another designer's bargain basement. All things being equal, how many "big" clients should you get? As many as you can handle, of course, but be careful not to put all your eggs in one basket.

You should set a limit on the percentage of income derived from any one client. If your firm stays afloat on the business of one (or a few) major accounts, it will mean disaster if those accounts pull out for any reason.

Maintain a broad client base. If the publishing industry is suffering, you know you're going to be in trouble if all of your business is in this sector. In the event of problems within a particular industry, a troubled economy, or the pull-out of a big client, you need to be flexible enough to regroup and work in another arena with a minimum of damage.

My business developed slowly (which was fine at the time). Accommodating my clients and providing the service promised was my goal. Satisfied clients will recommend you to others and this will help your business flourish. Happily, I still work with a number of my original clients.

Mary Ann Nichols, Nichols Graphic Design

Vicki Vandeventer

You Can Hire Me for Free(lance)

With one year as a production artist and six years as a college textbook designer behind her, Vicki Vandeventer went out on her own. "There was nowhere to go at the publishing company," she remem-

bers. "No room for growth beyond a certain point. I wanted new challenges." So, seeking to "learn the ropes and survive financially," Vandeventer began Vandeventer Graphic Design out of her Monterey, California, home in 1987.

She financed her first year of business with less than $2,000 in the bank. Fortunately, she was able to use much of her former employer's studio equipment. "All I bought initially was an answering machine and typewriter," she says. "I already had the drafting equipment." Shrewd bargaining and some good buys on used equip-

ment yielded additions to her office as her studio grew. "I bought a used copier from a client," Vandeventer states, "and another client paid for half of my fax machine when I needed it for one of their projects."

While getting started, Vandeventer made many sales calls and networked extensively. "I contacted college textbook publishers in the San Francisco Bay area," she says. "I let them know I was freelancing and arranged to show them

my portfolio. I also got a lot of jobs from former colleagues who had moved to other publishing companies."

Vandeventer has come to realize the great marketing potential in an effective self-promotion piece. To advertise her fledgling business, she sent out a brochure that read, "You can hire me for free," on the outside, with only ("lance") printed on the inside. Vandeventer enclosed her business card and followed up with requests for

Vandeventer has two versions of her "resuME" — the traditionally designed version shown here and another that uses a lively, provocative piece of clip art to attract clients looking for unconventional ideas and approaches.

portfolio reviews.

The clever promo was a rousing success and catchy enough to be acknowledged in a local design competition. "It worked so well," she tells us, "that I used the same idea in a new brochure series which was featured in the *HOW* 1991 self-promotion issue.

"As I diversify my clientele, moving away from textbook design and into a wider variety of projects, I will be doing more cold calls,"

says Vandeventer, acknowledging the important one-two punch of promotion and sales.

Vandeventer has encountered some resistance in her attempts to grow beyond the textbook market. "Many people don't seem to realize that a good designer can, with the right information, design just about anything. It's your skill at defining a problem — and your ability to creatively solve it, that you're really selling, not just your ability

to put together a book or brochure or whatever."

And so Vandeventer presses on. Despite the fact that she started out on a shoestring, was good enough to achieve national recognition, and is brave enough to promote her business in uncharted waters, this resourceful designer doesn't feel she is particularly courageous. "I just figured everything would work out, and it did."

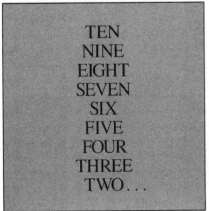

Vandeventer's 1991 self-promotion campaign consisted of a series of six brochures, three of which are shown here. The initial piece focuses on Vandeventer's motto, "You can hire me for free(lance)" which then appears on all subsequent pieces. One catchy, brightly colored brochure was sent every two months to current and prospective clients. Choosing to use her self-promotion budget for six simple brochures spread out over a year's time, rather than on one expensive promotion, kept Vandeventer on her clients' minds.

Dan Johnson

Building a Business on Service and Promotion

"Someone once said that a designer is a slow layout man with an ego," quips Dan Johnson. The Dayton, Ohio-based veteran has kept his sense of humor after some 33 years in the trade, including the trials and tribulations that come with running his own design studio, Art Direction Inc.

Johnson attended the Ringling School of Art in Sarasota, Florida. He ended up in Dayton after graduation and military service. He spent the next 11 years working for a Dayton design studio, learning every aspect of his trade by working his way up from studio gofer to art director.

In 1969 Johnson moved on to Pflaum Publishing, as he says, "to have complete control over design and because of my love for books and type design." In 1976, Pflaum closed its doors. Art Direction was born simply because Johnson needed a job.

Initially, he says, "Art Direction had one client and (consisted of) just me, working on my kitchen table." But Johnson was breaking even at the end of three months, and within a year business was too good for the fledgling enterprise to remain a home-based, one-man op-

eration. Today, his award-winning firm of nine does business on a national scale. But Johnson is quick to point out that this growth didn't

"just happen." He stresses the need for a marketing strategy and then describes his own approach as one of eliminating options. "To get clients I could be cheaper [than the competition]," he says. "But that doesn't seem to be a good approach. I have always done quality design and quality doesn't equate with cheap."

Johnson goes on to explain that by getting business through undercutting another designer's price, he would be setting himself up for accumulating fickle clients. "I could also wait around until [the client's] present supplier messes up so badly that he wants to try another designer," he says. "But I don't want clients that are fickle. I don't want clients that shop for price. I don't want clients that change suppliers with every job. I want loyal

clients because I'm a loyal supplier."

This strategy, he says, is based on a number of hypothetical tactics. "1) I could have an unusual talent . . . maybe I do a unique style of illustration. 2) Perhaps I have more experience in a certain area. For instance, a particular advertising niche like direct mail. 3) An opportunity may exist if I'm in a position to outservice a competitive design studio. 4) A change in personnel at a particular company can also open doors. We're starting with a clean slate," Johnson says, "The art buyer is new and now I have a fresh shot at their business."

To maintain a competitive edge, Johnson emphasizes the need for ongoing promotional efforts. "You must have a marketing and promotion plan," he explains. "You'll need to send direct mail frequently. Write so many letters today. Make a certain number of cold calls this week. Enter local shows and national competitions. It all goes together; you don't do just one part."

A veteran at effective direct mail promotions, Johnson has this advice to offer. "A nice mailer doesn't have to be elaborate. Creativity makes for a memorable promo." He cites effective use of typography or paper or "a new twist on an old idea." He also points out that "a creative promotion doesn't have to mean big bucks." Johnson advocates budgeting a specific amount for promotion on a yearly basis. "But I wouldn't put all of my money into one big shot," he cautions. "Black-and-white postcards, sent on a regular basis, can be tremendously effective." Johnson says he does monthly promotional mailings, "so when I walk in somewhere on a cold call, I'm not a complete stranger."

Johnson has some other cost-saving ideas. He advises keeping one's mailing list to a small, targeted group of perhaps 200 to 500 prospects. "If you have a small list you can do a lot of hand work yourself. Get fancy, have fun and save some money. You don't have to mail them out at the same time. If you're doing the work, and can only produce 20 a day, mail 20 a day."

Press overruns also offer self-promo potential. "If I'm doing a poster for a client, I'll cover the extra paper charges and simply overrun the piece," says Johnson. "I'll mail these out to prospects a month later to prevent a conflict of interest with my client. Along with the piece will be a note that says, 'Hi! I did this for XYZ.'"

On the subject of cold calling, Johnson has some strategies for maximizing one's time. He makes certain before he contacts any prospect, that he knows they are buying art. "You must first learn who the buyers are and know that they need design," he advises. "I wouldn't go

to ABC Widget Company, and they wouldn't be on my mailing list, unless I knew they were art buyers.

"If I'm visiting a regular client and I'm driving by ABC Widgets, I stop in. If I can't see the buyer, I'm on my way. I don't make a special trip—that would be a waste of time." Johnson notes that when cold calling, persistence pays off. "A couple of weeks later I'll stop in ABC Widgets again. After I've been there three of four times, and if there's any work, the art buyer might see me. I get a chance to show my portfolio."

Johnson also takes advantage of free time to do business. "A meet-

This early black-and-white self-promotional brochure exemplifies Johnson's idea of a "new twist on an old idea." Here, he uses the type of swatch brochure format used by paper and paint supply stores to show off the wide variety of logos designed by Art Direction Inc.

ing always takes me away from the drawing board, but I'm never at the board for lunch," he says. "A lot of business takes place at lunch because it's convenient, not because somebody wants to bum a meal. You can talk shop, sell or service, and eat—everybody's got to eat, right?"

Pointing out that serving your current clients is the best way to build a solid business, Johnson adds, "Service is being willing to work weekends and overtime and be there when clients need you. Make them feel they're the only customer that you have." He stresses the need for solving their problems. "They want someone who's going to say, 'It's OK, I can help you. I can fix it—I can make it better.' And even though you may have to jump off a few bridges to make it happen, you try to make it look very easy.

"Service takes time and costs money. Every design job will have many service calls, but good service means good sales."

This brochure targets clients who need presentation folders and brochures. Simple line art inside sketches the design options Art Direction can tailor to fit a client's special requirements. A carefully targeted mailer like this one often brings better results than a more general piece mailed haphazardly to possible clients.

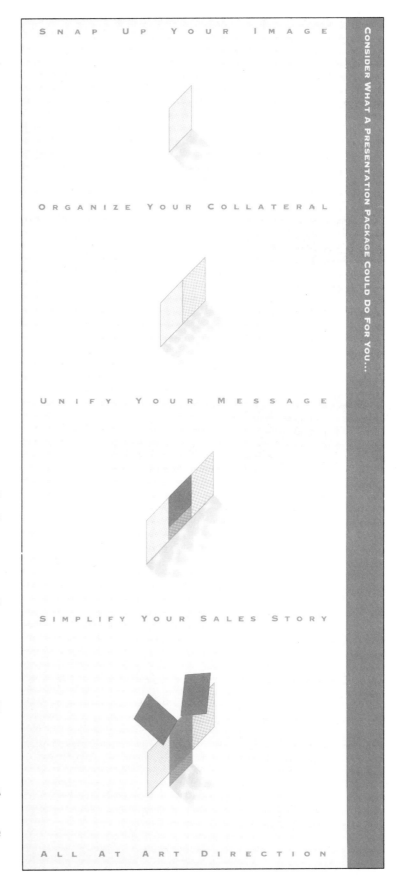

Practicing What We Preach— Promotion

Ed Hauben and Susan Tyrrell of Ruby Shoes Studio were coworkers at Illuminations, a giftware company in Cambridge, Massachu-

setts. Hauben was director of art and production; Tyrrell was the art director. Eventually, they decided that their considerable skills and services—honed over five years on staff—could be offered to outside clients. When, as Hauben says, it "became time to evolve into something else," they and another colleague left the fold. Their marketing strategy at that time was simple: Each would contact people they knew—vendors and suppliers— who might need design support. Then, when the shop doors opened, there would be work.

Their networking was a success. Each partner left the company at intervals every two months, within a six-month span. When they all got together, their small two-room studio had seven clients, none of which placed them in competition with their former employer. They even went back to work for Illuminations as an outside vendor. "When each of us left, there was work to be done. From the investment point of view, we didn't put any money into the business," Hauben says. "It was paying for itself from day one, June 1, 1984."

The other partner left two years later, but Hauben and Tyrrell maintained the firm. Today, Ruby Shoes specializes in creative promotional campaigns product and packaging design, including premiums and incentives (such as mugs and T-shirts).

So how do promotional experts promote themselves? "Networking and word of mouth have always been big for us," Hauben says. "We've had some recent success with cold calls, but 90 percent of our marketing effort has been through some kind of personal connection, once or twice removed—somebody suggests somebody. Through that chain of events we send out a cover letter with a package of materials and follow that up with a phone call. That's our style.

"We've entered (and won a few) national competitions, which is a very good way to become better known in the industry. But our own promotional efforts never seem to be enough. We struggle constantly, trying to allocate our limited resources between our existing workload and finding new business.

"We do a Christmas promotional T-shirt that we send to our clients, plus other holiday promos, too. For instance, a children's cal-

Ed Hauben's promotions for Ruby Shoes Studio play up their clever name based on the famous ruby slippers in *The Wizard of Oz*. Many pieces use a warm red for a second color, as does the newsletter shown here. This newsletter tells past, present and future clients about recent awards the studio has received and about "Toto," their new Mac II-based color graphics computer system.

endar we created was sent out at Thanksgiving saying 'Thanks for your trust in us and helping us be successful. When you're looking for creative services, think of us.'

"Being experts in promotional clubs, we decided to do a promotional series intended to create a Ruby Shoes Fan Club. We sent out a 'Club' promo flyer to former clients and new contacts offering a free consultation and special 'Club Member Only' benefits. We followed this up with a rolodex membership card, and then a phone call.

"Fortunately, the results of our promotional efforts over the past eight years have been successful. That's the good news, because it is both a liability and an asset," Hauben states. "Being part of a small studio, all of our staff wear many hats. I do the marketing and sales and oversee project coordination as well as do all of the proposal and contract writing. So, when I'm busy negotiating and writing contracts, our marketing effort takes a back seat." Over the years, Hauben has tried diligently to stay on top of it. If he has one recommendation or suggestion, he says, "It is that marketing and promotion be a high priority in any studio's business plan—that there be a consistent and continuous marketing effort to bring in work.

"If you're lucky you can find a project to sustain you over a long period of time," Hauben points

out. "That's happened for us, but seems to be less and less the reality now. The economic pressure these days is very great. Nothing is secure. We have very few clients who hire us on retainer. We're usually on a project basis. So this ongoing strategy of finding new clients is essential to the studio's survival."

Hauben feels that marketing and promotion must be "perceived as a priority—equal to creativity and technology. It must be funded. If possible, have somebody on it full-time. Come up with creative and innovative ways to introduce yourself to the client. Persistence is another key. The work is out there—you must pursue it."

Ruby Shoes Studio often does promotional series. This one invited former and prospective clients to join the Ruby Shoes Fan Club. The flyer describes the benefits of working with the studio and offers a portfolio review appointment and a free consultation in addition to the "official" membership card and newsletter.

Hauben and his partner, Susan Tyrrell, collaborated with freelance travel photographer Michael Levine on the creation and production of this high-quality calendar featuring Levine's work. Hauben and Tyrrell suggested that the theme of capturing the spirit of children around the world would be a timely topic, have wide appeal, and be a real possibility for commercial success. Feedback has been overwhelmingly positive, and the calendar won a Silver Award for Best Graphic Design from the Calendar Marketing Association. In exchange for Hauben and Tyrrell's investment of time and energy, Levine agreed to have a promotional statement about Ruby Shoes printed inside the cover of 250 calendars. These were given to Hauben and Tyrrell's friends and clients as gifts during the 1991 holiday season. They proved to be a very successful promotional device.

Credits and Permissions

Art Direction Inc. (pp. 73 right, 102 bottom, 104, 114-115)
© 1991 Art Direction Inc.

Adela Ward Batin (pp. 33, 81-82)
© 1990 Adela Ward Batin

Concrete (pp. 23-24, 42)
© Concrete. Photography (p. 24):
© 1989 Geof Kern

Nichols Graphic Design (pp. 89, 98)
© 1990 Juda Kallus/Mary Ann Nichols

Tom Nicholson (p. 13)
© 1991 IBM International Business Machines Corporation

Peg, Inc. (pp. 43-44)
© 1988-1992 Peg Esposito

Bennett Peji (pp. 15, 59-60)
© 1992 Bennett Peji

Pinkhaus (pp. 25-26)
© Pinkhaus Design Corp.

Mike Quon (pp.46-47)
© 1992 Mike Quon

Real Art Design Group, Inc.
(pp. 84, 85, 86 top, 97, 107)
© Real Art Design Group, Inc.

Ritter & Ritter, Inc. (pp. 27-28)
© 1990 Ritter & Ritter, Inc.

Ruby Shoes Studio (pp. 102 top, 117-118)
© Ruby Shoes Studio
Calendar (p. 118): © 1992 Les Enfants du Paradis/Michael Levine

Mike Salisbury (pp. 11-12, 105)
© Mike Salisbury

Shannon Designs (pp. 45, p. 68 bottom, p. 72 bottom, p. 73 left)
© 1991 Shannon Designs

Shapiro Design Associates (pp. 78-80, p. 72 top)
© Shapiro Design Associates
Symbol for Century Time Gems (p. 80): Martin Haggland - Microcolor, Inc.

Siebert Design Associates (pp. 57-58, p. 68 top, p. 86 bottom)
© 1990 Siebert Design Associates
photo (p. 57): Michael Wilson

Tharp Did It (pp. 9-10)
© Tharp Did It

Vandeventer Graphic Design
(pp. 112-113)
© 1987-1990 Victoria A. Vandeventer

Vie Design (pp. 95-96)
© Viemeister Design
photo: Denise Eagleson

Youngblood, Sweat & Tears
(pp. 61-62, p. 70 top)
© 1991 Youngblood, Sweat & Tears

Index